Nurturing Independent Thinkers

Working with an alternative curriculum

edited by

Mike Bosher & Patrick Hazlewood

Net

Published by Network Educational Press Ltd
PO Box 635
Stafford
ST16 1BF

© St John's School, Marlborough, Wiltshire 2005

ISBN-13: 978 1 85539 197 0
ISBN-10:   1 85539 197 X

Managing editor: Lynn Bresler – Lynn Bresler Editorial Services
Cover design: Marc Maynard – NEP
Design and layout: Marc Maynard – NEP
Photographs: Max More – St John's School, Marlborough, Wiltshire
Proofreader and indexer: Sue Lightfoot

Printed in Great Britain by Ashford Colour Press Ltd, Gosport, Hants.

Contents

Foreword

This book is a fascinating account of a learning journey – a journey that is still underway and one in which the school, its staff and its students are fellow travellers. This theme of a joint venture is important and indeed sets the tone for the whole book. The journey's purpose, to improve teaching and learning at St John's School, Marlborough, may be straightforward but I would not be the first person to say that the devil is in the detail. And so it has proved. The journey may not have always been clearly signposted, and there has been the occasional detour and diversion, but it is proving successful.

The phrase 'independent learning' is in danger of becoming a cliché and this makes St John's achievements all the more impressive because this is exactly what their students are becoming. They are acquiring the competences and abilities that will enable them to take responsibility for their own learning and to become independent learners. They are not dependent on their teachers to always tell them what to do and how to do it, they are learning when it is appropriate for them to make these decisions themselves – abilities they will need throughout the rest of their education and, indeed, their lives.

The book also clearly illustrates the impact of change on a school and the people in it. There is little if anything that has not been affected and an enormous management capability has been required of the school and its staff – and this is on top of the day-to-day teaching and administration. No small feat.

I have visited St John's School many times in the course of the RSA's *Opening Minds* project and I have always returned exhilarated and energized by the time I spent in the school. Reading this book has had the same effect.

Lesley James
Head of Education
RSA

Contributing authors

St John's School
& Community College
Marlborough

Dr Patrick Hazlewood, headteacher. During the 1980s he worked in Dorset, Devon, Cambridgeshire (head of science), Wiltshire (deputy head) and was involved in curriculum research and development most notably in the field of global education in the science curriculum working with the Centre for Global Education, University of York, WWF and the Council for Environmental Education.

Appointed to his first headship at Pool School and Community College, Cornwall (1991–1996), a school in challenging circumstances, he completed his PhD (Exon) in the successful management of secondary schools (1994). His second headship from 1996 provided the opportunity to build on this research and challenge the static and restrictive nature of the secondary curriculum and management practice.

Patrick Hazlewood BEd, MEd, PhD, FRSA

He has worked with the RSA from 1999 to date on the *Opening Minds* project (education for the 21st century), which places the learner at the centre of educational endeavour and redefines the role of the teacher, and he is currently a member of the RSA's curriculum advisory panel.

Dr Mike Bosher, deputy headteacher. He started teaching in 1967 at Guthlaxton Community College in Leicestershire, having graduated from Carnegies College for Physical Education in Leeds. He was very involved in both the teaching of physical education and in the Community Youth Education programme, together with the management committee of the community college. He moved to Marlborough in 1975 as head of physical education, became a head of year in 1978 and head of the Upper School in 1988. He was appointed as deputy headteacher in 1997. Mike has taught science throughout the 11–18 age range for the last 20 years and specializes in A/S and A2 biology.

As a member of the strategic management team he takes a full part in the management of the school, is the child protection co-ordinator, educational visits co-ordinator and is responsible for continuing professional development and school self-evaluation. He completed his Masters Degree at Oxford University in 1991 and his PhD in Education in 2001 with Bath University. His additional work in the school is related to Action Research and school innovation.

Mike Bosher Cert Ed, Dip Phys Ed,
BA, MEd, PhD

Kathy Pollard Dip Ed

Mrs Kathy Pollard, a principal tutor KS3 and director of primary partnerships. She started teaching in 1970 in Greater Manchester and soon became involved in the education of the whole child. She spent time in the 1970s developing appropriate courses and experiences across the whole ability range, and throughout the 70s and 80s she worked in a range of educational establishments at a senior level from infant through to adult education. She also worked on the entitlement curriculum 16–19 for the LEA and was involved in a variety of business and enterprise research projects.

More recently her career has been pastorally oriented with specific responsibility for transition KS2 to KS3. She became involved in the *Opening Minds* initiative, acting as principal evaluator for the St John's Curriculum. She was part of the management team responsible for the training of staff, and mapping and refinement of the new Curriculum, particularly regarding assessment and recording of progress. She has taken part in many seminars and conferences inspiring others from this country and abroad to develop their own solutions in light of St John's experience. She is currently involved in the personalized learning programme, particularly integrating the information from primary feeder schools into a useful and accessible resource.

Lyn Quantick Cert Ed

Mrs Lyn Quantick, KS3 strategy manager. During the early 1970s she taught in London and moved to Wiltshire in 1973. She worked at her village secondary school, moving to St John's in 1974, where she taught a variety of subjects – history, English, mathematics and PE. She was appointed to take charge of an initiative known as the Record of Personal Achievement for those in Years 10 and 11 in the latter part of the 1970s.

She has been a principal tutor within KS3 and now teaches English and the Alternative Curriculum.

Mr Richard Smith, a director of teaching & learning. He read for a degree in English at Royal Holloway, University of London (1992–1995) and went on to read for an MA in English Literature at King's College, University of London (1995–1996).

Working in the financial sector for a number of years he was based at Barclays Bank Head Office in the City, where he trained in multi-corporate banking and international currency (1997–2000). A dramatic change of career arose in 2000 when he retrained at Bath University as a secondary English teacher, before then joining the staff as a Key Stage 3 co-ordinator of English. Richard won a place on the Fast Track Teaching Programme in 2004.

Richard Smith BA (Hons), MA, PGCE

Dr Leslie Spencer. Leslie Spencer has been a teacher in the UK since 2000, teaching English and law. She also serves as a principal tutor for KS3–4. Previously, she taught Paralegal Studies at Notre Dame College, in Ohio, USA, where she also worked as an attorney.

Leslie Spencer BA, PGCE, LLD

Ms Imogen Willgress. Imogen started teaching infants in the mid 1970s and then emigrated to Western Australia where she taught a variety of age groups in mostly rural locations. She returned to Wiltshire in 1986 and started working straight away at the local village primary school. She then added part-time work at St John's School & Community College and for several years was teaching 4–16 year olds in the same week.

From 1993 Imogen has worked full time at St John's, combining English teaching with various roles from managing the library to being a head of year at KS3. She has spent some time studying part-time at Southampton University and graduated with an MA (Ed) in July 2000.

Imogen Willgress Cert Ed, MA

Chapter 1

The challenge for education in the 21st century

Patrick Hazlewood

Setting the scene

Imagine a happy, successful school set in a rural market town surrounded by countryside of outstanding natural beauty. The school is oversubscribed, results are very good and the school is highly regarded, providing very well for its children. Quality of teaching and learning, in the language of inspection, and success measured by outcome are very good. In such circumstances it is entirely possible that the same ingredients for 'success' will be reproduced year after year with the school striving to do at least as well as the previous year. Complacency is not an option but retaining a clear and vital philosophy of education leading to improvement in practice, to innovation, to living 'on the edge' is not encouraged. That at least was the case when the project to create a curriculum for the 21st century began.

The first stirrings of concern came after the Ofsted inspection of 2000 when the school was judged to be very effective. My view was that the staff were working as hard as they could, the children were performing at or around their target levels and any improvements in the future would very probably be by small increments. The far greater danger was that a decline in performance may set in. This effect, described by Handy (1994), suggests that all organizations go through phases of development and improvement. The danger comes in the replication of the measures for success when the world around has moved on and what made the organization successful may no longer be sufficient to maintain the upward trend. This phenomenon is as true of educational as it is of business and industrial organizations.

Over time it had become clear that the locus of endeavour within the school centred on the teaching and support staff. The children were compliant, for the most part, and were content to be led and told what to do. As normal adolescents most would get the work done *just* in time and the teacher would be the one under pressure to complete the assessment by the deadline. One of the defining characteristics of professional teachers is the generosity that they exhibit towards their charges, however irritating or lazy they may be! The coursework assessment, such an important component of exam accreditation in the latter part of the 20th century, was designed to allow students to demonstrate their skills outside the examination hall – but it became the burden that all teachers dread; yet another field of conflict in which quality of work and time became victims unless, of course, the teacher stepped in to the rescue. This is not to place the blame on the learner; coursework was yet another thing that 'they' did to you and eventually the game had to be played (but not without a bit of resistance!).

In 2001 the stark reality dawned. More of the same was not going to be in the interests of anyone, least of all the children. The curriculum and other aspects of the educational diet that formed the daily experience of school was probably little different to that encountered by the parents and, more worryingly, the grandparents! This is, perhaps, an exaggeration but one which raises the question, 'Is the National Curriculum a curriculum fit for the 21st century?' Or is it a curriculum in which subjects reinforce the notion of some learning being more important than others, of knowledge and understanding being of a higher order than the ability to apply learning. Much more disturbing is the failure to ask the question, 'Whose learning is it anyway?'

The curriculum from the perspective of the child is a strange affair. You go to school full of expectation and anticipation, full of enthusiasm for learning, ready to explore new ideas and to experience a challenge. What happens? Every hour the subject changes, you move 25 times a week and not one of the teachers you meet has any idea what each of the others has done with you. Some cover similar work on the assumption nobody else has done it, others forget that Year 7 in the secondary school is just that... it is the seventh year of formal education – and yet there seems to be a widely held view that the primary years didn't exist! A little exaggeration but not that much. For the child the curriculum becomes an incoherent jumble of 'subjects' with little planned interconnectivity; repetition, planned or otherwise, is increasingly evident; and personal ownership of the learning pathway is not a concept that the vast majority of children would recognize. Thirty years ago Stenhouse (1975) observed that 'schools take responsibility for planning and organizing children's learning. They try – and not very successfully – to give it direction and to maximize its effectiveness'. In the 21st century will it be any different? We have wandered into the new millennium with the relics of the past and an educational straitjacket still intact. If 'educational innovation' is about anything it must be about challenging individuals and systems to provide the very best learning opportunities and environment that we can.

Another example of these relics is the notion of 'homework'. It could be argued that this has been the single greatest source of conflict between parents and their children, between teachers and their students, and has been resented by generations as an imposition on their time at home (Hazlewood 2005). In the 21st century it is still there, promoted by the establishment without question. But does it really do what it is purported to do? Is it the way in which learning should be directed outside the classroom? Or is it an anachronism that effectively acts to reinforce the idea that learning at school is somehow different to learning at home?

This book makes the bold statement: *the approach to learning must be different*, the future of the human race may well depend on it. The far-reaching implications of failing to educate our children effectively, of failing to prepare them for a world in which the speed of change is becoming exponential and for a world in which uncertainty is the only certainty, will be dire indeed.

The turning tide

The establishment of a National Curriculum in 1988 was a direct response to the curriculum development pattern of the 1980s that saw a proliferation of courses designed to engage children and raise levels of motivation and achievement. Such courses, for example Mode 3 CSEs (Certificate of Secondary Education), were aimed towards those children who were not likely to achieve the higher level GCE. However, some of these courses did have an impact on the approach to GCE (Hazlewood 1985). The overall effect was that the experience of educational content could display a wide variation from area to area across the country. Hargreaves (2004a) identifies four factors that drive the curriculum: heritage, preparation, progression and motivation. In its original form the National Curriculum was designed to provide all children in England and Wales with a common curriculum experience that enforced both continuity and progression. Over the years modifications have recognized that motivation is a contributory factor to success in education and alterations have been made to both content and compulsion.

Through the 1990s a clear view from a range of sources in America, Canada, Australia and the UK began to emerge that suggested that the way things had been in education would not be how they would be in the future. Indeed the thrust was far more powerful; it began to challenge fundamental assumptions that hitherto remained relatively undisturbed. The rapid pace of human development witnessed through the 19th and 20th centuries began to look positively pedestrian compared with that of the current 'information age'. The 21st Century Learning Initiative (1997) presented a number of findings which radically altered the perspective of where education needed to go. The first area concerned the *personal construction of knowledge* which had shifted from the earlier behaviourist 'sum of the individual parts' perspective to a prevailing view that interactive relationships and a social construction of knowledge, meaning and connections were a better descriptor of human learning. This, connected with the second part of the shifting perspective, that *human evolution* was dependent on interaction with the environment which was, in turn, dependent on multiple forms of intelligence that helped make sense of that environment, called into question the way in which learners were taught. The traditional views of how the *brain* actually functioned were also open to radical alteration and in consequence *ideas about learning* needed to evolve from simple self-organization towards a collaborative, interpersonal and social problem-solving activity.

In parallel with shifting perspectives on the nature of learning the 1990s became the decade which hosted a wide-ranging debate about the nature, organization and management of schools in the 21st century. Caldwell and Spinks (1988) in their 'gestalt for schooling in the knowledge society' identified seven areas for radical change:

- **connectedness in the curriculum:** the need for dramatic changes in teaching and learning methodology, allied with 'new technology', would challenge the very idea of subject boundaries;

- **workplace transformation:** the move away from the traditional school day and approaches to human resource management to create an entirely new framework for school operation, meeting the needs of the learner not the institution;

- **school fabric and globalization:** electronic networking, independent and individual learning would require a radical shift in the structuring of the fixed learning environment;

- **professionalism and great teaching:** the organization of learning, approaches to learning, and range of people involved in the process of learning, would be more complex than ever before and would elevate the role of teachers. The ability to challenge every learner would become the real challenge of teachers in the 21st century;

- **teams and pastoral care:** accepting that human learning is a collaborative and interpersonal activity, really effective learning requires effective pastoral care. The concept of the team in every aspect of the workplace becomes fundamental to the learning environment;

- **cyber policy, access and equity:** equal access to ICT for all must be an entitlement principle for all learners:

- **virtual schools:** virtual learning and learning network organization becomes a reality in the knowledge society.

This last part of the gestalt is particularly important: the central idea that learning can occur anywhere and anytime, rather than the 20th-century 'truth' that you go to school to learn. The false implication is that this is the place for formal education and anything else is somehow accidental! Of course this a simplistic exaggeration but a deliberate one. If we are to move education into the 21st century then *all* learning must be valued; the artificial barrier between learning at school and learning at home (homework) should not exist. However, school remains important as the sponsor of learning. It provides the place that Ellyard (1997) describes as a centre for collaborative learning. He goes on to say that 'learning is most effective if it occurs in an environment which makes the learning relevant…to the experience and expectations of the learner'.

It is at this point that the thinking around education in the 1990s began to merge. Gardner (1983) proposed a range of intelligences that enabled learners to learn. These 'multiple intelligences' (MI) help us to understand how people learn and to accommodate preferred learning styles. Sternberg (1997) makes the interesting distinction between *what people can do* (MI) and *what they prefer to do* (style). One of the fundamental problems with education in schools, and probably in most organizations, through the 20th century, is that certain styles of learning are valued more than others and learners whose style doesn't fit with the organizational preference tend to do less well. Sternberg describes *learning style* as 'a way of thinking' and *an ability* as 'how well the person does something'. The crucial issue is that success or failure in school depends not on the person's ability but on whether the approach to learning matches the preferred learning style of the individual. Much of schooling to date, certainly at secondary level, has been a 'one size fits all' approach.

A view from the RSA

In 1998 the RSA (Royal Society for the encouragement of Arts, Manufactures and Commerce) published a major report entitled *Redefining Work* (Bayliss 1998a) supported by a further report in the same year, *Redefining Schooling* (Bayliss 1998b). The view proposed by these influential reports was that the world of work had changed dramatically as the 20th century drew to a close and would continue to do so in the 21st century. The dawn of the era of information and communications technology (ICT) had become, within a few short years, the driving force behind the future evolution of work and the global economy. The pace would only be likely to increase and the challenges facing workers in the 21st century were almost certain to be very different to those that their predecessors in the 20th century had experienced. The need for flexibility, adaptability, transferability in terms of acquisition of knowledge and skills would be primary requirements of all employees. The reports also reflected the view that, in this new world, the education structure at the turn of the new millennium was essentially 19th century in philosophy and organization. The National Curriculum so forcefully implemented in 1988 (Maclure 1988) had, in my view, failed to address the future needs of both learners and society.

Redefining Work called for a full integration of information and communications technology into education. While this was belatedly addressed by the Labour government in 1997 the unpreparedness of the education system was such that a massive inertia against change existed. The manner of persuasion used by the government was also at odds with the purpose for encouraging ICT in schools. Setting targets and outcome expectations did not accord well with creating capable learners who used ICT as an aid to learning. Once again the failure to provide a coherent philosophy to support curriculum change threatened to draw schools away from the fundamental question about what the curriculum for the 21st century should look like.

The second 'driving force' recommended by the RSA was the *competence driven curriculum*. The curriculum staggering out of the 20th and into the 21st century was fundamentally influenced by assessment and examination. The concentration on subject knowledge, rather than on the specific skills and competences needed to function effectively in the world, dominated the curriculum and the examination system. The assessment of these skills was non existent and therefore low in the priorities of the education system. The RSA argued forcefully that this failure to prepare the children of today for the adult world of tomorrow would be to disadvantage both the learner and by consequence the society in which they lived and worked. The repeated message from employers to schools was that the employees emerging from schools were not properly equipped for the workplace. I would add at this point that I do not believe that the purpose of education is to act as a preparation for the world of work but it must be a consideration in the education of the fully rounded person.

The RSA therefore proposed three main areas in the remit of redefining the curriculum:

- re-engineering education around a competence based curriculum;
- analysis of the impact of ICT on schooling;
- and what the competence based curriculum might look like and how it might be assessed.

Through a series of four seminars in 1998, for Fellows of the RSA from a wide range of professional backgrounds, the RSA sought to establish a consensus on these three areas. The first area of curriculum re-engineering attracted little in the way of consensus partly because educational change was perceived to be driven by politicians and educational practitioners and therefore discouraged a wider view of what education could/should look like, and partly because little consensus could be achieved even with that opportunity! In the second area again little real coherence in the views of participants could be achieved. It was agreed to be of vital importance but how to bring about transformation into an ICT centred curriculum culture was uncertain. Through much discussion a general acceptance of the competence base for a curriculum was established; it left many more questions than answers not least issues of assessment and how long-term change can be managed in the education system.

In 1999 the RSA launched an exploratory project to test the competence based curriculum. The title contained more than a hint of excitement and challenge; when *Opening Minds: education for the 21st century* began there was the potential for a radical re-focusing of education. The competences that formed the backbone of the 'new curriculum'

1. learning to learn

2. citizenship

3. relating to people

4. managing situations

5. managing information

seemed in one sense obvious but without substance (full details of the RSA competences are given in Appendix 3). The real challenge was to construct a curriculum that created the opportunities for the application of these competences to dramatically alter the child's experience of learning in school, significantly raise the quality of that experience and prepare our learners for the 21st century. The challenge was also complex; it raised issues of convincing teachers, governors and parents that this was a project that would enhance the children's learning experience. For the teachers there were also issues around *how* and *what*, those fundamental matters of practicality that without clear answers no philosophical proposal can move forward. Visions are all very well but in the end they must deliver in practice; the quality of educational experience *must* be better; no learner must be disadvantaged by the process; no parent should be left concerned by the 'experiment'; and no teacher should feel professionally exposed by their involvement. It is one of those cases where everyone involved must be a winner. Failure cannot be an option.

Currently there are over 100 schools in England using, or proposing to use, the competences as the framework for planning their curriculum in Year 7. This number includes middle and secondary schools plus a couple of special schools. Some secondaries have integrated all the National Curriculum subjects, others have used the humanities and arts subjects as the focus for their competence work. The number of schools looking towards this curriculum as a 'solution' is expanding rapidly.

The experience to date of schools using the RSA competences is that student motivation is much improved, and that behaviour and attendance also improve. There is a great deal of work involved for teachers, but they too report that they enjoy using the competences. Through using an integrated curriculum they get to know their students better and have developed a better 'learning relationship' with their classes.

The following chapters detail the journey and story of how one school created a curriculum for the 21st century. At the heart of our ambition was the intention of creating a curriculum that would develop capable, competent and confident learners, learners who could face challenges, relate well to people, be effective problem solvers and who could manage information skilfully and with purpose. Most importantly we wanted to create the educational environment in which learners loved learning.

Chapter 2

From dependence to independence

Mike Bosher and Patrick Hazlewood

The first part of this chapter is written with a view to giving the reader a feel for the school in its geographical and organizational context, to enable the reader to understand how the management and organization of the school changed to meet new educational demands, and how the curriculum in the lower school was developed using the environment and resources in the surrounding locality.

A pen portrait of St John's

St John's is a rural mixed non-selective 11–18 comprehensive school set in the Kennet Valley on the outskirts of the market town of Marlborough in Wiltshire. The adjoining Savernake Forest, Avebury stone circle, the Iron Age site at Silbury Hill and the white horse country of the Pewsey Vale, all serve as a backdrop.

It was established in 1550 under the auspices of the Church of St John and during the 18th century it became known as Marlborough Grammar School. After several moves to different sites in the town, it became established in 1962 on the fringe of the main retail and housing areas. In another part of the town, Marlborough Secondary Modern School was established just after the Second World War. In 1975, the two schools combined to become St John's School with the sites split by a journey of 1.2 miles.

The school re-designated itself as a Community College in 1997 as a statement of support to the community it serves and became a Technology College in 1998. It has a catchment area of approximately 125 square miles and a feeder catchment of 13 primary schools. The school student population at the present time is 1,500 with a sixth form of 290 students offering 27 A/S and A2 subjects including Classics, Classical civilization and law. The nearest secondary school in any direction is 8 miles away, and St John's provides a sixth form for students from the nearest of those schools who live in the area of the Pewsey Vale.

The Upper School took the name of a previous headteacher, A.R. Stedman, author of *The History of Marlborough Grammar School* (1944), and became known as the Stedman site, while the Lower School was named the Savernake site after the extensive royal hunting forest which overlooks the town.

In 2005 the school is awaiting planning permission to move within the next 18 months onto the Stedman site with a proposed new development costing in excess of £20 million which will provide a state-of-the-art educational facility offering a flexible teaching and learning environment exclusively designed to meet the needs of education for the 21st-century student.

St John's Lower School

At the present time, the school population is split between the two sites with Key Stage 3 on the Lower School Savernake site and Key Stages 4 and 5 on the Upper School Stedman site. In order to facilitate effective teaching and learning, and to maximize resources and facilities, a nomadic existence is experienced by all staff and many students as they move between sites. The school has a permanent coach and driver on hand to transport students between the sites with approximately 2,500 student movements a week. It is a requirement of all staff who teach in the school that they should do so across both the ability and age range and, in consequence, staff move between sites, often 2–4 times a day.

A further consequence of this constant movement is that no staff and few students have a base that they can call 'home'. No teacher has a classroom allocated to them and many have a filing system which is the back seat of their car! Many staff meetings take place as snatched conversations in transit. This nomadic existence instils a degree of organization into everyone but leads to emotional and physical fatigue by the end of each week. Despite these apparent difficulties, the school enjoys an excellent academic reputation, being named by HMCI in 1997 as 'one of the country's top comprehensive schools providing education of a very high standard' (HMI Report 1997).

St John's Upper School

Achievements at GCSE are 70 per cent grades 5+A*-C and A2 results achieved averaged out at 312 points per student in 2004.

Nurturing Independent Thinkers

Working with an alternative curriculum

edited by

Mike Bosher & Patrick Hazlewood

Network**Educational**Press

Published by Network Educational Press Ltd
PO Box 635
Stafford
ST16 1BF

© St John's School, Marlborough, Wiltshire 2005

ISBN-13: 978 1 85539 197 0
ISBN-10:   1 85539 197 X

Managing editor: Lynn Bresler – Lynn Bresler Editorial Services
Cover design: Marc Maynard – NEP
Design and layout: Marc Maynard – NEP
Photographs: Max More – St John's School, Marlborough, Wiltshire
Proofreader and indexer: Sue Lightfoot

Printed in Great Britain by Ashford Colour Press Ltd, Gosport, Hants.

Contents

Foreword

This book is a fascinating account of a learning journey – a journey that is still underway and one in which the school, its staff and its students are fellow travellers. This theme of a joint venture is important and indeed sets the tone for the whole book. The journey's purpose, to improve teaching and learning at St John's School, Marlborough, may be straightforward but I would not be the first person to say that the devil is in the detail. And so it has proved. The journey may not have always been clearly signposted, and there has been the occasional detour and diversion, but it is proving successful.

The phrase 'independent learning' is in danger of becoming a cliché and this makes St John's achievements all the more impressive because this is exactly what their students are becoming. They are acquiring the competences and abilities that will enable them to take responsibility for their own learning and to become independent learners. They are not dependent on their teachers to always tell them what to do and how to do it, they are learning when it is appropriate for them to make these decisions themselves – abilities they will need throughout the rest of their education and, indeed, their lives.

The book also clearly illustrates the impact of change on a school and the people in it. There is little if anything that has not been affected and an enormous management capability has been required of the school and its staff – and this is on top of the day-to-day teaching and administration. No small feat.

I have visited St John's School many times in the course of the RSA's *Opening Minds* project and I have always returned exhilarated and energized by the time I spent in the school. Reading this book has had the same effect.

Lesley James
Head of Education
RSA

Contributing authors

St John's School
& Community College
Marlborough

Dr Patrick Hazlewood, headteacher. During the 1980s he worked in Dorset, Devon, Cambridgeshire (head of science), Wiltshire (deputy head) and was involved in curriculum research and development most notably in the field of global education in the science curriculum working with the Centre for Global Education, University of York, WWF and the Council for Environmental Education.

Appointed to his first headship at Pool School and Community College, Cornwall (1991–1996), a school in challenging circumstances, he completed his PhD (Exon) in the successful management of secondary schools (1994). His second headship from 1996 provided the opportunity to build on this research and challenge the static and restrictive nature of the secondary curriculum and management practice.

Patrick Hazlewood BEd, MEd, PhD, FRSA

He has worked with the RSA from 1999 to date on the *Opening Minds* project (education for the 21st century), which places the learner at the centre of educational endeavour and redefines the role of the teacher, and he is currently a member of the RSA's curriculum advisory panel.

Dr Mike Bosher, deputy headteacher. He started teaching in 1967 at Guthlaxton Community College in Leicestershire, having graduated from Carnegies College for Physical Education in Leeds. He was very involved in both the teaching of physical education and in the Community Youth Education programme, together with the management committee of the community college. He moved to Marlborough in 1975 as head of physical education, became a head of year in 1978 and head of the Upper School in 1988. He was appointed as deputy headteacher in 1997. Mike has taught science throughout the 11–18 age range for the last 20 years and specializes in A/S and A2 biology.

Mike Bosher Cert Ed, Dip Phys Ed,
BA, MEd, PhD

As a member of the strategic management team he takes a full part in the management of the school, is the child protection co-ordinator, educational visits co-ordinator and is responsible for continuing professional development and school self-evaluation. He completed his Masters Degree at Oxford University in 1991 and his PhD in Education in 2001 with Bath University. His additional work in the school is related to Action Research and school innovation.

Kathy Pollard Dip Ed

Mrs Kathy Pollard, a principal tutor KS3 and director of primary partnerships. She started teaching in 1970 in Greater Manchester and soon became involved in the education of the whole child. She spent time in the 1970s developing appropriate courses and experiences across the whole ability range, and throughout the 70s and 80s she worked in a range of educational establishments at a senior level from infant through to adult education. She also worked on the entitlement curriculum 16–19 for the LEA and was involved in a variety of business and enterprise research projects.

More recently her career has been pastorally oriented with specific responsibility for transition KS2 to KS3. She became involved in the *Opening Minds* initiative, acting as principal evaluator for the St John's Curriculum. She was part of the management team responsible for the training of staff, and mapping and refinement of the new Curriculum, particularly regarding assessment and recording of progress. She has taken part in many seminars and conferences inspiring others from this country and abroad to develop their own solutions in light of St John's experience. She is currently involved in the personalized learning programme, particularly integrating the information from primary feeder schools into a useful and accessible resource.

Lyn Quantick Cert Ed

Mrs Lyn Quantick, KS3 strategy manager. During the early 1970s she taught in London and moved to Wiltshire in 1973. She worked at her village secondary school, moving to St John's in 1974, where she taught a variety of subjects – history, English, mathematics and PE. She was appointed to take charge of an initiative known as the Record of Personal Achievement for those in Years 10 and 11 in the latter part of the 1970s.

She has been a principal tutor within KS3 and now teaches English and the Alternative Curriculum.

Mr Richard Smith, a director of teaching & learning. He read for a degree in English at Royal Holloway, University of London (1992–1995) and went on to read for an MA in English Literature at King's College, University of London (1995–1996).

Working in the financial sector for a number of years he was based at Barclays Bank Head Office in the City, where he trained in multi-corporate banking and international currency (1997–2000). A dramatic change of career arose in 2000 when he retrained at Bath University as a secondary English teacher, before then joining the staff as a Key Stage 3 co-ordinator of English. Richard won a place on the Fast Track Teaching Programme in 2004.

Richard Smith BA (Hons), MA, PGCE

Dr Leslie Spencer. Leslie Spencer has been a teacher in the UK since 2000, teaching English and law. She also serves as a principal tutor for KS3–4. Previously, she taught Paralegal Studies at Notre Dame College, in Ohio, USA, where she also worked as an attorney.

Leslie Spencer BA, PGCE, LLD

Ms Imogen Willgress. Imogen started teaching infants in the mid 1970s and then emigrated to Western Australia where she taught a variety of age groups in mostly rural locations. She returned to Wiltshire in 1986 and started working straight away at the local village primary school. She then added part-time work at St John's School & Community College and for several years was teaching 4–16 year olds in the same week.

From 1993 Imogen has worked full time at St John's, combining English teaching with various roles from managing the library to being a head of year at KS3. She has spent some time studying part-time at Southampton University and graduated with an MA (Ed) in July 2000.

Imogen Willgress Cert Ed, MA

Chapter 1

The challenge for education in the 21st century

Patrick Hazlewood

Setting the scene

Imagine a happy, successful school set in a rural market town surrounded by countryside of outstanding natural beauty. The school is oversubscribed, results are very good and the school is highly regarded, providing very well for its children. Quality of teaching and learning, in the language of inspection, and success measured by outcome are very good. In such circumstances it is entirely possible that the same ingredients for 'success' will be reproduced year after year with the school striving to do at least as well as the previous year. Complacency is not an option but retaining a clear and vital philosophy of education leading to improvement in practice, to innovation, to living 'on the edge' is not encouraged. That at least was the case when the project to create a curriculum for the 21st century began.

The first stirrings of concern came after the Ofsted inspection of 2000 when the school was judged to be very effective. My view was that the staff were working as hard as they could, the children were performing at or around their target levels and any improvements in the future would very probably be by small increments. The far greater danger was that a decline in performance may set in. This effect, described by Handy (1994), suggests that all organizations go through phases of development and improvement. The danger comes in the replication of the measures for success when the world around has moved on and what made the organization successful may no longer be sufficient to maintain the upward trend. This phenomenon is as true of educational as it is of business and industrial organizations.

Over time it had become clear that the locus of endeavour within the school centred on the teaching and support staff. The children were compliant, for the most part, and were content to be led and told what to do. As normal adolescents most would get the work done *just* in time and the teacher would be the one under pressure to complete the assessment by the deadline. One of the defining characteristics of professional teachers is the generosity that they exhibit towards their charges, however irritating or lazy they may be! The coursework assessment, such an important component of exam accreditation in the latter part of the 20th century, was designed to allow students to demonstrate their skills outside the examination hall – but it became the burden that all teachers dread; yet another field of conflict in which quality of work and time became victims unless, of course, the teacher stepped in to the rescue. This is not to place the blame on the learner; coursework was yet another thing that 'they' did to you and eventually the game had to be played (but not without a bit of resistance!).

In 2001 the stark reality dawned. More of the same was not going to be in the interests of anyone, least of all the children. The curriculum and other aspects of the educational diet that formed the daily experience of school was probably little different to that encountered by the parents and, more worryingly, the grandparents! This is, perhaps, an exaggeration but one which raises the question, 'Is the National Curriculum a curriculum fit for the 21st century?' Or is it a curriculum in which subjects reinforce the notion of some learning being more important than others, of knowledge and understanding being of a higher order than the ability to apply learning. Much more disturbing is the failure to ask the question, 'Whose learning is it anyway?'

The curriculum from the perspective of the child is a strange affair. You go to school full of expectation and anticipation, full of enthusiasm for learning, ready to explore new ideas and to experience a challenge. What happens? Every hour the subject changes, you move 25 times a week and not one of the teachers you meet has any idea what each of the others has done with you. Some cover similar work on the assumption nobody else has done it, others forget that Year 7 in the secondary school is just that... it is the seventh year of formal education – and yet there seems to be a widely held view that the primary years didn't exist! A little exaggeration but not that much. For the child the curriculum becomes an incoherent jumble of 'subjects' with little planned interconnectivity; repetition, planned or otherwise, is increasingly evident; and personal ownership of the learning pathway is not a concept that the vast majority of children would recognize. Thirty years ago Stenhouse (1975) observed that 'schools take responsibility for planning and organizing children's learning. They try – and not very successfully – to give it direction and to maximize its effectiveness'. In the 21st century will it be any different? We have wandered into the new millennium with the relics of the past and an educational straitjacket still intact. If 'educational innovation' is about anything it must be about challenging individuals and systems to provide the very best learning opportunities and environment that we can.

Another example of these relics is the notion of 'homework'. It could be argued that this has been the single greatest source of conflict between parents and their children, between teachers and their students, and has been resented by generations as an imposition on their time at home (Hazlewood 2005). In the 21st century it is still there, promoted by the establishment without question. But does it really do what it is purported to do? Is it the way in which learning should be directed outside the classroom? Or is it an anachronism that effectively acts to reinforce the idea that learning at school is somehow different to learning at home?

This book makes the bold statement: *the approach to learning must be different*, the future of the human race may well depend on it. The far-reaching implications of failing to educate our children effectively, of failing to prepare them for a world in which the speed of change is becoming exponential and for a world in which uncertainty is the only certainty, will be dire indeed.

The turning tide

The establishment of a National Curriculum in 1988 was a direct response to the curriculum development pattern of the 1980s that saw a proliferation of courses designed to engage children and raise levels of motivation and achievement. Such courses, for example Mode 3 CSEs (Certificate of Secondary Education), were aimed towards those children who were not likely to achieve the higher level GCE. However, some of these courses did have an impact on the approach to GCE (Hazlewood 1985). The overall effect was that the experience of educational content could display a wide variation from area to area across the country. Hargreaves (2004a) identifies four factors that drive the curriculum: heritage, preparation, progression and motivation. In its original form the National Curriculum was designed to provide all children in England and Wales with a common curriculum experience that enforced both continuity and progression. Over the years modifications have recognized that motivation is a contributory factor to success in education and alterations have been made to both content and compulsion.

Through the 1990s a clear view from a range of sources in America, Canada, Australia and the UK began to emerge that suggested that the way things had been in education would not be how they would be in the future. Indeed the thrust was far more powerful; it began to challenge fundamental assumptions that hitherto remained relatively undisturbed. The rapid pace of human development witnessed through the 19th and 20th centuries began to look positively pedestrian compared with that of the current 'information age'. The 21st Century Learning Initiative (1997) presented a number of findings which radically altered the perspective of where education needed to go. The first area concerned the *personal construction of knowledge* which had shifted from the earlier behaviourist 'sum of the individual parts' perspective to a prevailing view that interactive relationships and a social construction of knowledge, meaning and connections were a better descriptor of human learning. This, connected with the second part of the shifting perspective, that *human evolution* was dependent on interaction with the environment which was, in turn, dependent on multiple forms of intelligence that helped make sense of that environment, called into question the way in which learners were taught. The traditional views of how the *brain* actually functioned were also open to radical alteration and in consequence *ideas about learning* needed to evolve from simple self-organization towards a collaborative, interpersonal and social problem-solving activity.

In parallel with shifting perspectives on the nature of learning the 1990s became the decade which hosted a wide-ranging debate about the nature, organization and management of schools in the 21st century. Caldwell and Spinks (1988) in their 'gestalt for schooling in the knowledge society' identified seven areas for radical change:

- **connectedness in the curriculum:** the need for dramatic changes in teaching and learning methodology, allied with 'new technology', would challenge the very idea of subject boundaries;

- **workplace transformation:** the move away from the traditional school day and approaches to human resource management to create an entirely new framework for school operation, meeting the needs of the learner not the institution;

- **school fabric and globalization:** electronic networking, independent and individual learning would require a radical shift in the structuring of the fixed learning environment;

- **professionalism and great teaching:** the organization of learning, approaches to learning, and range of people involved in the process of learning, would be more complex than ever before and would elevate the role of teachers. The ability to challenge every learner would become the real challenge of teachers in the 21st century;

- **teams and pastoral care:** accepting that human learning is a collaborative and interpersonal activity, really effective learning requires effective pastoral care. The concept of the team in every aspect of the workplace becomes fundamental to the learning environment;

- **cyber policy, access and equity:** equal access to ICT for all must be an entitlement principle for all learners:

- **virtual schools:** virtual learning and learning network organization becomes a reality in the knowledge society.

This last part of the gestalt is particularly important: the central idea that learning can occur anywhere and anytime, rather than the 20th-century 'truth' that you go to school to learn. The false implication is that this is the place for formal education and anything else is somehow accidental! Of course this a simplistic exaggeration but a deliberate one. If we are to move education into the 21st century then *all* learning must be valued; the artificial barrier between learning at school and learning at home (homework) should not exist. However, school remains important as the sponsor of learning. It provides the place that Ellyard (1997) describes as a centre for collaborative learning. He goes on to say that 'learning is most effective if it occurs in an environment which makes the learning relevant…to the experience and expectations of the learner'.

It is at this point that the thinking around education in the 1990s began to merge. Gardner (1983) proposed a range of intelligences that enabled learners to learn. These 'multiple intelligences' (MI) help us to understand how people learn and to accommodate preferred learning styles. Sternberg (1997) makes the interesting distinction between *what people can do* (MI) and *what they prefer to do* (style). One of the fundamental problems with education in schools, and probably in most organizations, through the 20th century, is that certain styles of learning are valued more than others and learners whose style doesn't fit with the organizational preference tend to do less well. Sternberg describes *learning style* as 'a way of thinking' and *an ability* as 'how well the person does something'. The crucial issue is that success or failure in school depends not on the person's ability but on whether the approach to learning matches the preferred learning style of the individual. Much of schooling to date, certainly at secondary level, has been a 'one size fits all' approach.

A view from the RSA

In 1998 the RSA (Royal Society for the encouragement of Arts, Manufactures and Commerce) published a major report entitled *Redefining Work* (Bayliss 1998a) supported by a further report in the same year, *Redefining Schooling* (Bayliss 1998b). The view proposed by these influential reports was that the world of work had changed dramatically as the 20th century drew to a close and would continue to do so in the 21st century. The dawn of the era of information and communications technology (ICT) had become, within a few short years, the driving force behind the future evolution of work and the global economy. The pace would only be likely to increase and the challenges facing workers in the 21st century were almost certain to be very different to those that their predecessors in the 20th century had experienced. The need for flexibility, adaptability, transferability in terms of acquisition of knowledge and skills would be primary requirements of all employees. The reports also reflected the view that, in this new world, the education structure at the turn of the new millennium was essentially 19th century in philosophy and organization. The National Curriculum so forcefully implemented in 1988 (Maclure 1988) had, in my view, failed to address the future needs of both learners and society.

Redefining Work called for a full integration of information and communications technology into education. While this was belatedly addressed by the Labour government in 1997 the unpreparedness of the education system was such that a massive inertia against change existed. The manner of persuasion used by the government was also at odds with the purpose for encouraging ICT in schools. Setting targets and outcome expectations did not accord well with creating capable learners who used ICT as an aid to learning. Once again the failure to provide a coherent philosophy to support curriculum change threatened to draw schools away from the fundamental question about what the curriculum for the 21st century should look like.

The second 'driving force' recommended by the RSA was the *competence driven curriculum*. The curriculum staggering out of the 20th and into the 21st century was fundamentally influenced by assessment and examination. The concentration on subject knowledge, rather than on the specific skills and competences needed to function effectively in the world, dominated the curriculum and the examination system. The assessment of these skills was non existent and therefore low in the priorities of the education system. The RSA argued forcefully that this failure to prepare the children of today for the adult world of tomorrow would be to disadvantage both the learner and by consequence the society in which they lived and worked. The repeated message from employers to schools was that the employees emerging from schools were not properly equipped for the workplace. I would add at this point that I do not believe that the purpose of education is to act as a preparation for the world of work but it must be a consideration in the education of the fully rounded person.

The RSA therefore proposed three main areas in the remit of redefining the curriculum:

- re-engineering education around a competence based curriculum;

- analysis of the impact of ICT on schooling;

- and what the competence based curriculum might look like and how it might be assessed.

Through a series of four seminars in 1998, for Fellows of the RSA from a wide range of professional backgrounds, the RSA sought to establish a consensus on these three areas. The first area of curriculum re-engineering attracted little in the way of consensus partly because educational change was perceived to be driven by politicians and educational practitioners and therefore discouraged a wider view of what education could/should look like, and partly because little consensus could be achieved even with that opportunity! In the second area again little real coherence in the views of participants could be achieved. It was agreed to be of vital importance but how to bring about transformation into an ICT centred curriculum culture was uncertain. Through much discussion a general acceptance of the competence base for a curriculum was established; it left many more questions than answers not least issues of assessment and how long-term change can be managed in the education system.

In 1999 the RSA launched an exploratory project to test the competence based curriculum. The title contained more than a hint of excitement and challenge; when *Opening Minds: education for the 21st century* began there was the potential for a radical re-focusing of education. The competences that formed the backbone of the 'new curriculum'

1. learning to learn

2. citizenship

3. relating to people

4. managing situations

5. managing information

seemed in one sense obvious but without substance (full details of the RSA competences are given in Appendix 3). The real challenge was to construct a curriculum that created the opportunities for the application of these competences to dramatically alter the child's experience of learning in school, significantly raise the quality of that experience and prepare our learners for the 21st century. The challenge was also complex; it raised issues of convincing teachers, governors and parents that this was a project that would enhance the children's learning experience. For the teachers there were also issues around *how* and *what*, those fundamental matters of practicality that without clear answers no philosophical proposal can move forward. Visions are all very well but in the end they must deliver in practice; the quality of educational experience *must* be better; no learner must be disadvantaged by the process; no parent should be left concerned by the 'experiment'; and no teacher should feel professionally exposed by their involvement. It is one of those cases where everyone involved must be a winner. Failure cannot be an option.

Currently there are over 100 schools in England using, or proposing to use, the competences as the framework for planning their curriculum in Year 7. This number includes middle and secondary schools plus a couple of special schools. Some secondaries have integrated all the National Curriculum subjects, others have used the humanities and arts subjects as the focus for their competence work. The number of schools looking towards this curriculum as a 'solution' is expanding rapidly.

The experience to date of schools using the RSA competences is that student motivation is much improved, and that behaviour and attendance also improve. There is a great deal of work involved for teachers, but they too report that they enjoy using the competences. Through using an integrated curriculum they get to know their students better and have developed a better 'learning relationship' with their classes.

The following chapters detail the journey and story of how one school created a curriculum for the 21st century. At the heart of our ambition was the intention of creating a curriculum that would develop capable, competent and confident learners, learners who could face challenges, relate well to people, be effective problem solvers and who could manage information skilfully and with purpose. Most importantly we wanted to create the educational environment in which learners loved learning.

Chapter 2

From dependence to independence

Mike Bosher and Patrick Hazlewood

The first part of this chapter is written with a view to giving the reader a feel for the school in its geographical and organizational context, to enable the reader to understand how the management and organization of the school changed to meet new educational demands, and how the curriculum in the lower school was developed using the environment and resources in the surrounding locality.

A pen portrait of St John's

St John's is a rural mixed non-selective 11–18 comprehensive school set in the Kennet Valley on the outskirts of the market town of Marlborough in Wiltshire. The adjoining Savernake Forest, Avebury stone circle, the Iron Age site at Silbury Hill and the white horse country of the Pewsey Vale, all serve as a backdrop.

It was established in 1550 under the auspices of the Church of St John and during the 18th century it became known as Marlborough Grammar School. After several moves to different sites in the town, it became established in 1962 on the fringe of the main retail and housing areas. In another part of the town, Marlborough Secondary Modern School was established just after the Second World War. In 1975, the two schools combined to become St John's School with the sites split by a journey of 1.2 miles.

The school re-designated itself as a Community College in 1997 as a statement of support to the community it serves and became a Technology College in 1998. It has a catchment area of approximately 125 square miles and a feeder catchment of 13 primary schools. The school student population at the present time is 1,500 with a sixth form of 290 students offering 27 A/S and A2 subjects including Classics, Classical civilization and law. The nearest secondary school in any direction is 8 miles away, and St John's provides a sixth form for students from the nearest of those schools who live in the area of the Pewsey Vale.

The Upper School took the name of a previous headteacher, A.R. Stedman, author of *The History of Marlborough Grammar School* (1944), and became known as the Stedman site, while the Lower School was named the Savernake site after the extensive royal hunting forest which overlooks the town.

In 2005 the school is awaiting planning permission to move within the next 18 months onto the Stedman site with a proposed new development costing in excess of £20 million which will provide a state-of-the-art educational facility offering a flexible teaching and learning environment exclusively designed to meet the needs of education for the 21st-century student.

St John's Lower School

At the present time, the school population is split between the two sites with Key Stage 3 on the Lower School Savernake site and Key Stages 4 and 5 on the Upper School Stedman site. In order to facilitate effective teaching and learning, and to maximize resources and facilities, a nomadic existence is experienced by all staff and many students as they move between sites. The school has a permanent coach and driver on hand to transport students between the sites with approximately 2,500 student movements a week. It is a requirement of all staff who teach in the school that they should do so across both the ability and age range and, in consequence, staff move between sites, often 2–4 times a day.

A further consequence of this constant movement is that no staff and few students have a base that they can call 'home'. No teacher has a classroom allocated to them and many have a filing system which is the back seat of their car! Many staff meetings take place as snatched conversations in transit. This nomadic existence instils a degree of organization into everyone but leads to emotional and physical fatigue by the end of each week. Despite these apparent difficulties, the school enjoys an excellent academic reputation, being named by HMCI in 1997 as 'one of the country's top comprehensive schools providing education of a very high standard' (HMI Report 1997). Achievements at GCSE are 70 per cent grades 5+A*-C and A2 results achieved averaged out at 312 points per student in 2004.

St John's Upper School

The management solutions to the issues raised earlier

On a more global school front, there was, as we started the 2005 academic year, a move forwards in philosophical thinking. The management of the school is in the collegiate hands of many more people than it was in 1996 and feels comfortable, with decision making much more widely spread across the areas of responsibility. The move now is for the strategic management team to engender a new perspective and outlook in educational vision making. The strategy is to move the directors down the transformational road taken years ago by the headteacher. The school has, in 2005, appointed four directors of Teaching and Learning whose sole responsibility is to raise both the quality of teaching and learning in the school, but also to totally embed the concept of shared practice. The school now needs the managers in the middle to engage in the process of leadership rather than just management. The management of the day-to-day activities of the directorate are to be delegated to the deputy director. This will release the director from those traditional tasks and allow more time and energy for the forward thinking and planning processes necessary to take the directorate forwards. This is now necessary as the effects and impact of the competency based learning approach is now in Year 9. What must happen now is that while the curriculum initiative remains in the domain of Years 7 and 8, it is essential that the skills and competences developed in these early years are encouraged to continue into the students' learning experiences in Key Stage 4 and 5. For this to happen effectively, the directors need to be planning ahead, creating schemes of work and developing teaching strategies that will enable this to happen. Hence the need for leadership and vision, not just management at director level, to become the expected norm.

Chapter 3

The beginning of a curriculum revolution

Lyn Quantick with Imogen Willgress

Early days

The images of water, stones and ripples come to mind when I look back at the development of the Integrated Curriculum over the past four years, that, and the fortunate state of affairs that put me in the right place at the right time in order to be a member of the team that was to float this new concept.

Imagine being told by your headteacher that the school would be 'throwing the Key Stage 3 National Curriculum out of the window'. Well, that was what the staff were challenged with during 2001. This paralleled the thinking of Lawton (1973) who had said:

> *...The assumption is often made that if something has been taught for a number of years by schools it must inevitably remain the same.*

The progression and development of the new curriculum started quietly enough, almost by stealth. The first stirrings began in the autumn term of 2000. The teaching staff had been introduced to Howard Gardner's ideas based around the understanding of multiple intelligences and how such knowledge would empower both staff and pupils. This was further built upon by a visit to school on a staff development day by Professor Guy Claxton, the exponent of the Learning to Learn movement, who, in one morning, was able to excite and promote his ideas on aiding learning (see page 36). Guy Claxton's lecture had sown seeds of interest in the processes involved in learning. We found ourselves speaking about key skills, accelerated learning, preferred learning styles, multiple intelligences, emotional intelligences, *Opening Minds* competences, learning to learn, 'lifelong learning' and 'thinking outside the box'. Thus the first two aspects of what was to become our new curriculum thinking were already, if we did but know it, in place.

Learning to learn

In his lecture on 'Schooling for the Learning Age', Professor Guy Claxton analysed the processes we employ when we meet new challenges and outlined to us the three stages of resilience, resourcefulness and reflection that lead to enhancing learning power. **Resilience** refers to the ability to be able to cope with problems without getting upset, to persevere when something is difficult, to recover from setbacks, to be able to feel uncertain without feeling insecure, to build a learning stamina and to also be aware of emotional intelligence. **Resourcefulness** is basically having a variety of learning strategies to call on, knowing when and how to use those strategies and generally knowing what to do when you don't know what to do. It also involved developing all one's learning skills and being aware of the inner mental/emotional process of learning. The final 'R' is **reflection**. We certainly did plenty of reflecting as we planned for the future. We thought about our own learning, our strengths and weaknesses, and our responsibility for our own learning and at the same time tended to self-evaluate our contributions.

In January 2001 the challenge, given by the head, was for all staff to justify their subject's contribution to the curriculum. The initial challenge focused on Year 8; the hypothesis posed was that Year 8 was a waste of time! This was based on subject content duplication, repeating work from previous years without being aware of the fact and the observation that Year 8 was the year where a learning 'slump' set in. Questions, such as, for example – 'Were the lessons challenging enough?' 'Was this a year when pupils could ease up and slow down?' 'Was valuable time lost as both teachers and pupils relaxed between the stress years of induction and transfer in Year 7 and SATs in Year 9?' – allowed teachers to quietly reflect and, if necessary, justify what was being taught. It would allow them to consider where the subjects might overlap the whole curriculum and therefore where there may be opportunities for collaboration and joint planning for curriculum delivery. For the first time since the introduction of the National Curriculum the staff were given the freedom to think 'outside the box'. Could some areas of the school curriculum be taught by teams of teachers? Did some subjects offer the chance to 'bleed in' to a wider, topic-based educational approach and so complement each other?

The direct result of these musings in a practical sense led to subject areas promoting, within their own directorates and on the wider stage to the whole school, a series of 'wow' lessons, incorporating the recent educational ideas we had started to discover and explore. (The 'wow' term came from the enthusiastic responses that became a feature of this sharing of practice.) Slowly but surely the emphasis was moving from *what* we were teaching to *how* it was done. Teachers were still bound and constrained by the National Curriculum but at last had been given the freedom to openly discuss and, if needed, to change the style of delivery and even the content. The first faltering steps had begun, had we but realized it…

In March 2001 there was a 'twilight' staff development session to discuss the direction of 'the curriculum in the future' at St John's. This pulled together and allowed the assessment of many of the initiatives that had already been started: GCSE accelerated single sciences, accelerated maths, key skills, multiple intelligences, learning to learn, and finally, the RSA *Opening Minds* project. Underpinning the discussion was the premise that in order for pupils to be educated in the broadest sense, with the necessary skills to take them through a lifetime of learning, we needed to be quite clear about what was really relevant in each subject area despite the straitjacket of the

National Curriculum. This would require, without breaking the law with respect to the National Curriculum, a re-engineering of the curriculum, starting with Year 7 and involving all subject areas, which would firstly have to justify what *they* could offer towards the learning of pupils at Key Stage 3. Teachers had the freedom to examine what might be considered the barriers to an education fit for a citizen in the 21st century, at the same time the process of examining their subject in depth and justifying what it could offer to a 21st-century learner.

Jumping ahead temporarily, it is clear that the government has begun to question what education in schools need to focus on. In January 2004, David Miliband, then Minister of State for School Standards, in his speech to the North of England Conference, stated that:

 The challenge for education in the 21st century is to give the common basics of citizenship and working life to every pupil, while developing and nurturing the unique talents of each pupil.

And so the pieces were almost in place. In April 2001 the head asked for volunteers who might be interested in looking at the ideas that had been quietly percolating through the corridors of St John's. Those early volunteers looked at the ways in which the timetable and curriculum could be structured. The sense of youngsters following a learning journey was firmly established and the content and delivery was likened to travelling with a courier who guided them through the learning process. Subjects were in fact secondary, they were merely the vehicle to deliver the main thrust of the *Opening Minds* idea, which was to embed the competences and so produce a firm foundation for learning that would not just be useful throughout the life of a student in school, but indeed, would be the backbone of that child's learning development throughout life itself.

It was vital that every area of the curriculum was represented if a new curriculum was to be devised. Luckily this was virtually the case.

Getting going

What was being asked of those who volunteered to take part in the creation of a skills based curriculum for the pilot third (that is, three out of the nine classes) of the Year 7 intake for September 2001 cannot be underestimated. If we could have anticipated the workload over the next year, alongside all the usual demands that face a full-time teacher, we all might well have thought twice before taking up the challenge ahead.

In June the 21 volunteers were taken off timetable and out of school for two days of extensive brainstorming ready to kick off in September. That gave just about three months to effect a change that was to take the Key Stage 3 curriculum demands and come up with a replacement that would be infinitely more appropriate for moving the education of our students into the 21st century – a mammoth task, but one that was exciting, stimulating and energizing. It uniquely allowed colleagues a rare insight into each other's curriculum areas and encouraged the sharing of ideas – everyone had an equal stake in this creation.

No one could be expected to deliver a whole year of study, across the entire selection of subjects, within the limited timeframe. It was therefore decided that the most efficient way forward would be to split into teams of teachers from various subject areas, who would then prepare a scheme of work for a six-week module. This was a chance to make the task ahead 'do-able'. Great care had to be taken to ensure that in using the new initiatives of *Opening Minds*, multiple intelligences, learning to learn and Daniel Goleman's (1995) emotional literacy, as well as taking the opportunity of 'cleaning up' and tightening the curriculum, we did not lose sight of the imperative that being innovative is of no use whatsoever if the end result is that the students would not benefit.

En masse we then set about the creation of the module titles, six in all (see opposite). The decision had been taken to develop the work as an Action Research project with both internal and external evaluators. Three tutor groups out of the nine forms of entry were selected at random. Given that there would be three teaching groups within the pilot, teachers divided into three teams with specialists from all of the disciplines represented. However, there were subject gaps of one sort or another within every team – if you choose as a specialist teacher to see it that way. This therefore meant that, in keeping the teaching teams small, there would be a need to take that leap and work 'outside the box'. One team, for example, delivered their module using a scientist who also taught the class mathematics and German; another team used a teacher to deliver English, history, RE and drama. It is worth noting that some subjects found the whole process difficult to work with and adapt to; it was ambitious in the first place to try to incorporate all subjects. PE made considerable efforts to 'fit into' the modules, while modern foreign languages were working diligently to adapt materials so they could be used. It was especially hard for that subject area to impart vital basic knowledge through the topic approach. It was also difficult, if not impossible, for them to deliver their lessons in the target language and also keep the 'story' element of the module going. At least it was still possible to concentrate on delivery of the *Opening Minds* competences even if that did feel like a compromise. All of this needless to say created a huge learning curve for the staff concerned, but teachers both inside and outside of the project were generous in their offers of materials and advice.

Each team would be responsible for the creation and implementation of initially one module, a second module would need to be prepared during the autumn term to start in the New Year. The year's curriculum was to be based on the competences identified by the RSA.

The guiding principle behind the competence based curriculum is that it is all about process, not outcome. The learning journey is the key to its success, not the arrival. There is no doubt therefore that the Key Stage 3 Strategy, that was beginning to be implemented countrywide, could only enhance our work and encourage us in the direction we had chosen to take for our Year 7 students. A significant amount of effective strategies had been disseminated and cascaded throughout the school following training days that had been held by Wiltshire LEA for Key Stage 3. From the school's point of view this has complemented and further embedded the idea of a skills based curriculum. For St John's the focus on Key Stage 3 couldn't have happened at a more opportune moment.

In order to make the most of the limited time at our disposal, and to allow us breathing space to develop and change the scheme of work if needed, it was decided that each team would teach each of the pilot classes on a carousel system. We would teach one of the classes through the six-week module and then the class would move on to the next team, we, meanwhile, would teach the same module to the second and third classes. This would give time to 'fine tune' the modules and iron out any problems that had not been foreseen; also schemes could be adjusted, adding 'extras' that may well have come from the students themselves. The curriculum expected students to be prepared to take the reins in aiding and extending their own learning. Teachers were not seen as 'experts' and if questions needed to be answered the students were as likely to find them as the member of staff.

As the second modules were devised by each team, it was possible to see where there were gaps in the curriculum that needed to be filled, both within each team's module demands as well as those wider issues that arose across the pilot classes as a whole. There was also great merit in having a second chance to re-visit classes as the second modules got underway. It allowed us to see the development of the students as the Integrated Curriculum continued to unfold. It also gave the teams a chance to evaluate the knowledge that was being delivered and, if needed, the chance to add or remove anything that was extraneous to the delivery of the curriculum. Probably the most difficult task to pin down was, and still remains, the mapping and assessment of the students' progress.

After much discussion, and in order to give as wide an umbrella to work under as possible, the module titles were devised, the second module from each team would complement and build on the strengths of the first and there would be the chance to look sympathetically at all of them as a whole. The modules were designed so that every team member knew exactly what each other would be delivering each lesson. Therefore it relied upon the support the teams would offer each other in the delivery of the module. Each lesson would be a step along the road of the student's learning. Each teacher was to be seen as a guide or facilitator along the learning pathway. At the end of each lesson all that changed was the torch bearer. There needed to be a smooth route planned from teacher to teacher without any recourse to note the subjects individually. If the students, because of their growing confidence as independent learners, felt the need to move the lesson away from the expected route, then that too would be acceptable; in fact, it was delightful to meander along a slightly different route as it then showed that the students did indeed have a stake in their own learning. So, the Integrated Curriculum (as it was initially called) was born, the module titles being:

Being Unique   **Higher, Faster, Stronger**

Making the News   **Going Places**

Forests   **Counting the Cost**

What had to be kept at the forefront of the decision making was what it was that individual subjects needed to cover by the end of Year 7 and also what was to be expected by the end of the Key Stage itself. This certainly focused individuals on the demands of their subject in relation to the requirement to create a skills based curriculum. It encouraged us each to examine what would be necessary to complete the traditional Year 7 demands from within individual subjects. Teachers needed to be prepared to let go of an area of knowledge if it could be covered within the module more effectively by another subject specialist in the team. Freedom was also given to pull on board anything that would enhance the curriculum and stretch the students. Teaching would indeed be 'outside the box', no longer were there to be restraints on using in Year 7 work seen as traditionally covered by Year 8, or for that matter, Year 9 and upwards. What would now be considered was how best within the classroom we could deliver specific skills in each lesson. The curriculum for the 21st century would only be as strong and coherent as the sum of its parts… we *had* to keep communication open between ourselves; the successes and the failures of the scheme all needed to be highlighted and discussed.

The loss of subject control felt by directors was, understandably, of real concern to them; they had lost their control and expertise over a third of the year, and would be responsible for results both at Key Stage 3 and later at GCSE. They had to watch, some sceptically, from the sidelines. There was in fact only one director within the volunteers. The other directors had to put their trust and confidence in the innovative members of their directorate to see that their subject requirements were met. Perhaps until the pilot year was underway, they, like many, still felt that a school's success rested on its examination results rather than the foundation year of a comprehensive school. Certainly, such a debate still continues. It is after all, quite a change in mindset to put greater weight and emphasis behind the lowliest year in a school; being able to accept that a solid foundation in Year 7, created by students gaining a love of learning by giving them the skills they would require to easily adapt and change, would ultimately deliver a more confident learner who would more readily be able to meet the changing demands of the curriculum as they moved through the Key Stages. This was, for some at the time, and even now, a step too far! Unfortunately, our tight schedule meant there was little time for discussion or philosophical debate. This is perhaps where the new curriculum failed to get across to all members of staff. Or perhaps the unexpected success itself, right from the start, may have been the problem.

The school staff was originally simply invited to volunteer enthusiastic pioneers, who then moved forward with the project. Unexpected obstacles or logistic problems, not only during the period of the pilot, but also during the next two years as it continued to evolve, at times called for quick solutions or changes of direction. To those not involved in the overview it undoubtedly looked as if those heading the project didn't know what they were doing. There was also the problem that, as those team members became more involved and convinced about the 'product' they were trialling, a sense of exclusivity, a 'them and us' scenario evolved.

A visit from an HMI in 2002 led him to write:

 ...the integrated curriculum has had a significant impact on pupil achievement, teaching and learning styles, classroom climate, behaviour, levels of attendance, attitudes towards homework and the development of pupils' social skills and self-esteem.

(confidential memorandum)

....so why was it that the staff were so hard to get on board? This has caused the greatest heart searching but the answer, retrospectively, is clear.

Teachers are a stubborn breed; tell them to do something without the chance for healthy debate and they immediately feel it can't or shouldn't happen. On reflection, the school missed the vital link of discussion and a chance for staff to air their doubts and concerns; these in turn could have been assuaged through talking openly and without the fear of being a labelled a dinosaur. However, those of us deeply involved and committed to the new curriculum failed to realize that others might not be as enthusiastic as we were. As the *Opening Minds* project was the embodiment of the headteacher's personal and professional belief, colleagues probably felt obliged to comply even if they felt it was either alien to their style of teaching, or, even more fundamentally, not the right way forward. As this was a child-centred style of teaching there was no doubt in everyone's mind that such a method of teaching was expected to be employed by all teachers if they were to feel a secure member of the St John's staff. The feeling for some that they had a metaphorical gun in their back would have done little to 'open the minds' of some teachers.

It is possible for teachers to accuse the strategic management team of foisting onto overworked staff a curriculum that they had no part in creating. It is also clear that lack of involvement within the continued development of the Integrated Curriculum led some teachers to show a less than real commitment to the scheme. Furthermore when it might fail to produce the expected results teachers could then use the 'I told you so' argument as their crutch against the failure to make it work as expected.

On reflection we could be accused of imposing the curriculum by using the power-coercive strategy. As time was so limited, we therefore did not explain the strengths of the new curriculum clearly enough (though there was no shortage of results, statistics or outside evaluators to further champion its success). Perhaps we needed to realize that for those looking in as it were from the outside, maybe seeing parts of their traditional curriculum either being axed or hijacked within the modules, some teachers felt powerless, or ignored or frustrated by changes over which they had lost control. Teachers needed to be fully conversant with the positive aspects of the curriculum, but it is easy to sound such an 'expert' that it daunts staff or else so patronizing that they will switch off; it has not been an easy course to follow. Shout of the successes and it sounds like conceit; when things don't develop as expected it's a stick to beat the changes with. Offer staff development days for whole-school training and be accused of spending too much time on the pet project of the moment; don't offer staff support and be seen as casting staff adrift in a sea of confusion! Help! For both sides of the coin...

Additional elements

Tools of the Trade

In order to allow the pilot classes to have what was hoped would be a 'kick start' at the beginning of September, a two-week induction scheme of work was devised, outside of the modules, that would go some considerable way towards arming the students with specific skills that would then be universally called upon during the course of their time throughout Key Stage 3. This would help save space within the school day, thus avoiding repeating in too many lessons the same pieces of information they would need, whatever the lesson happened to be. This two-week segment of the school year was aptly called 'Tools of the Trade' (see page 42) and was vital in allowing all students to start from the same position, to feel secure and ready to face the challenge of the modules themselves. It is interesting to note that once the Integrated Curriculum was accepted as the way we would teach the Year 7 cohort at St John's the Tools of the Trade introduction was dropped for the following two years. This has now been re-introduced as it was seen as such a useful start to the year as it was able to enhance the teaching of the six modules.

During these two weeks, of course, we would not only concentrate on, for example, showing students how to log on to the computer network, take notes or access information, but also how to develop the competences that underpin the whole curriculum. This was done by organizing tasks that required the students to take that first tentative step towards relying on each other, thinking things through, gaining each other's trust and respect, as well as making it quite clear what the expectations were to be in an Integrated Curriculum classroom. Certainly it was vital to instil a real sense of respect for each other in the classroom, otherwise the students would have felt subdued and reticent to contribute.

Another major cause of success was that teachers simply expected their classes to aim high; very high expectations were always at the forefront of their learning, as was the freedom to experiment

TOOLS OF THE TRADE – Start of term 1

The term will begin with just Year 7 in school for the first day. This will give them the chance to re-familiarize themselves with the layout and routines before the other students return.

This module will build upon the Induction activities which focused on relating to people, managing situations and team building. Incidentally, there are a lot of problem solving and learning to learn activities.

The Tools of the Trade module will start with an assembly and PowerPoint presentation to the students at the start of the year.

All teachers	Learning styles and how to make the best use of them – refer to the students' MIs (multiple intelligences) and keep referring to them in the early weeks. These need to be made explicit in **each subject area**. Classroom expectations. Standards of presentation. Behaviour policy. **Identify all students on the special needs register.**
English	Literacy and Communication. Library skills 2x1 hour sessions – accessing information. Spelling policy. Group-work skills, e.g. A day in the life of ... to include research skills, interviewing and formats for reporting back. Story-telling and re-telling, primary sources, secondary sources. Silent reading ability. Classroom expectations coping with new ideas, e.g. background music, forming groups, moving the furniture round when needed.
Maths	Classroom expectations. Coping with new ideas, e.g. forming groups, moving the furniture round when needed. Numeracy. Mental maths, 66 test on tables.
Science	Classroom expectations. Coping with new settings, forming groups, moving the furniture/equipment round when needed. Accessing and using information: health and safety around school, personal responsibility, science and DT rooms in particular. Establishing safe working practices, e.g. science experiments. Problem-solving activities, hands-on where possible.
Drama	Classroom expectations. Relating to people. Circle time and establishing the rules for successful circle time.
Art	Communication skills. Classroom expectations. Problem-solving activities, hands-on where possible.
DT	Classroom expectations. Coping with new ideas, e.g. background music, forming groups, moving the furniture round when needed. Numeracy. Problem-solving activities, hands-on where possible.
MFL	Classroom expectations. Coping with new ideas, e.g. background music, forming groups, moving the furniture round when needed. Relating to people. Citizenship. Group-work skills, e.g. A day in the life of ... to include research skills, interviewing and formats for reporting back.
RE	Classroom expectations. Coping with new ideas, e.g. forming groups, moving the furniture round when needed. Citizenship.
Humanities	Classroom expectations. Coping with new ideas, e.g. background music, forming groups, moving the furniture round when needed. Accessing and using information.
PE	Classroom expectations. Coping with new ideas, e.g. background music, forming groups, moving the furniture round when needed. Accessing and using information.
Music	Classroom expectations. Coping with new ideas, e.g. background music, forming groups, moving the furniture round when needed.
ICT	Classroom expectations. Code of conduct. Using the network – accessing their work area, log-on, passwords, code of conduct.

[named staff]	A trip to @Bristol.
[named staff]	Making it Real – a citizenship activity which lasts for a day spent with the tutor, one band at a time.
Tutors	<ul><li>How students should learn, the classrooms and learning environments, catering and social facilities, break times and lunchtimes.</li><li>Listening skills.</li><li>Emotional intelligence and raising student self-esteem.</li><li>Making friends, self and body image, leading on to bullying and name calling.</li><li>Extended learning expectations and how to establish good habits.</li><li>Learning support. Learning clubs and workshops.</li><li>Who's who, know your school, how systems work.</li><li>The power of positive thinking, setting goals and 'dreaming' – developing ambition, positive mental attitude, printing positive thinking messages.</li></ul>

without a fear of being ridiculed by their peers if things did not work out as they had hoped. Freedom to try, without ridicule, was a very powerful tool during that first year; certainly the teachers found this to be so, just as much as the students.

The Book

Always, as the pilot unfolded, it was of paramount importance that at no time would the students be disadvantaged by their changed curriculum. The problem of mapping the work covered by the students was an especially difficult one. If, as a vital part of the student's acquisition of knowledge it was possible and moreover likely, that they would move off of the planned path the teaching team was expecting them to follow, it was vital that everyone knew what had happened.

It wasn't enough that the changed lesson was known to the teacher concerned and the class involved, such information needed to be passed on to all teachers, so that the 'diversion' could be built upon by the rest of the team, which in turn may well have led to other alterations throughout the module. If unrecorded it would have been feasible that major sections of knowledge that needed to be delivered might be lost in the enthusiasm of a new route.

How best to record the lesson by lesson information, regarding both the competency and subject topic covered, required careful thought. First it was considered using a laptop for each team. However, St John's is a split site school and the thought of racing between sites 1.2 miles distant then rushing to a central point to collect a laptop was not a sensible option. The solution was certainly not high tech but allowed us to put the onus for its success onto the students themselves. A monitor in each of the three classes would be responsible for giving to their teacher at the start of the lesson a learning log, universally known as 'The Book', that they would fill in. It also gave instant feedback about what had happened in earlier lessons that day that a teacher might possibly wish to build upon. At the end of the lesson the monitor would check the teacher had written the required information and then take it off with the class, to the next teacher. It is testament to the development of their personal confidence that the monitors had no trouble in making sure we regularly filled it in. The students themselves saw this as a vital part of their lessons and if the log was missing became proactive about finding it without making it a job for 'teacher', a sure sign that they were becoming responsible for their own learning!

The Book in practice

Completing 'The Book' was an enormous undertaking for a teacher who was probably commuting to the upper school (1.2 miles away) at break. Although it was a very useful mapping tool it proved to be unworkable and was abridged drastically. One of the things that did become obvious was that if the team had had time to discuss and produce the module then the 'log' was more easily understood and consequently members of staff were able to support each other more positively. Discussing the 'log' with the class is a valuable tool because it soon becomes evident exactly what they are gaining from the module. They love to share the experiences they have had in other lessons and give their viewpoint on the relevance of certain parts of the topic. I have gone into a class with a lesson prepared and then changed it totally after discussion of the 'log' and it is that opportunity for spontaneity and 'seizing the moment' which is so exciting in this approach.

Naturally while I describe this situation as being 'exciting' I am perfectly aware that some of my colleagues would see it negatively because it does not give them time or opportunity to reflect and plan in detail prior to the lesson. We are all coming from our different unique positions in life and while we are working towards shared objectives it does not mean that we achieve this in identical ways. It is important to respect the differences between us and not automatically expect the next teacher to continue with the activities in the log just because the students are having a good time and enjoying what they are working on. On the other hand, when the designated student has forgotten to get the 'log' filled out or has left it somewhere and cannot find it a frustrating situation can develop as the next teacher dashes into the lesson and wants to check exactly what has been covered before launching into whatever she has prepared. Still, it is an opportunity for students to be encouraged to take responsibility for their learning and resolve the situation one way or another and gain from the experience.

There was the further bonus that we had a 'live' document that showed us at any time how the modules were performing and, even more importantly, ensuring that there was an accurate overview of the curriculum that was unfolding for each class. One of the ideas behind the pilot was that lessons would respond to the needs and demands of the students; however it was important to avoid three classes with three totally different learning experiences in Year 7, creating difficulties in later years relating to subject knowledge and concept understanding.

Listening to the students

The decision was taken to keep movement about the school for the project students to a minimum. This, it was felt, would build on conditions that they were used to during their Key Stage 2 experience and make them feel more secure in the 'big' school. However, they didn't agree! They wanted to discover the DT workshops and the science labs, they enjoyed the music room and longed to go inside the drama studio. However, this could not always happen as timetabling is a complicated business and rooms had often been allocated to other classes.

An inkling of the relationship between the students and their teachers is that we did take on board their requests and tried to meet them where possible. For example, we had chosen to avoid all mention of 'subjects' within the lessons. When a class moved on to another teacher that's all it was to be, not a case of moving into a history lesson or an English lesson. In order to keep the learning journey as broad and flexible as possible we decided that they would distinguish lessons only by the teacher's initials, thus avoiding the pitfall of writing out a named subject. A decision therefore had been taken to expect the students to write on paper that could then be filed, in order to make their work notes as flexible as possible. This it was felt would give power to the sense of a story of learning unfolding throughout the module, without recourse to sorting through a variety of exercise books which might interrupt the flow. How wrong could we be! The students, who soon showed just how motivated they were in their work, did not take at all kindly to writing on paper. As far as they were concerned they felt it was untidy and messy and did little to make them feel proud of their efforts. Well, that *was* an area that could be changed, and needless to say they were immediately the happy owners of exercise books that could be neatly kept or used as notebooks depending on the tasks set, identified on the front by the teacher's initials only. We had listened to our customers!

Teaching in this way was much more a partnership with our students, the didactic teacher had indeed disappeared. We did not spoon-feed the classes we taught; they were given the means to find out knowledge or information for themselves. It certainly required those involved to take a leap of faith and change a teaching style that they might have been comfortable with for, in some cases, a very long time. Within the framework of the project teachers really did open themselves up to be tested alongside their students. The idea that the teacher was always right, knew all the answers and rigidly planned the direction of each lesson was gone. This could be dangerous; it wasn't. It was a chance to share knowledge and delight in a broader, planned programme of learning that was no longer hidden within the restrictive skirts of the National Curriculum. Learning was no longer to be within the constraints of a Year 7 curriculum, if they moved into Year 9 territory or wanted to struggle with a concept that would keep a Year 11 student on their toes that would be fine. We did not need to break the law to make it work. In fact, David Hargreaves, chief executive of the Qualifications and Curriculum Authority, answered the challenge laid down by Patrick Hazlewood by saying at the launch of the *Opening Minds* project in London in 2001:

 Patrick isn't really ditching the National Curriculum at all. He is doing something much more commendable; he is seeking to turn a curriculum for teaching into a curriculum for learning by means of a new pedagogy for learning.

A member of staff once remarked to me that as she passed by the classroom she had guessed that it was an Integrated Curriculum lesson because of the noise; she didn't mean it was loud and unruly, she meant it as a compliment to the learning that was going on inside and I accepted it as such. This of course for some is the crux of the matter. Having the confidence to allow useful dialogue in the classroom, that isn't time wasting chatter; for some it is a hard rope to balance on.

There will be times when discrete teaching has to take place; this must happen if progress is to be made. However, it is important to remember that the main aim of any lesson is still the competency that is to be selected, the subject is secondary to that and becomes the vehicle to move it forward. There was a very complicated job to be done to ensure that the knowledge that was necessary for building on subject development sat comfortably underneath the umbrella of the modules. The modern foreign language and mathematics directorates in particular had a difficult task to manage in order to complement the rest of the team but also, in doing so, making sure that their subject development was able to continue to move forward as they would normally expect.

It is certainly true that some subjects have been easier to incorporate into the Integrated Curriculum, either because the teaching styles already used by that subject area are sympathetic to the project, or because the development of the subject allows it to be rather more adaptable to the new curriculum. Other subject areas have found it hard to fit in. That doesn't mean that they haven't, what it does mean is that some directorates have had to take their subject apart and have then re-written entire schemes of work in order to find the most suitable package to fit within the Integrated Curriculum model.

First year of pilot project (2001/2002)

Prior to the start of the project in September 2001 the headteacher had spoken to the parents of the new intake, explaining the detail behind the national pilot that St John's was to trial. Whether it is testament to the project's virtues, or Dr Hazlewood's rhetoric, who can say, but the idea was enthusiastically received at each meeting. He explained that the pilot would involve three of the nine classes, so allowing the rest of the year to act as the control group. He also stressed that no student would be disadvantaged by the scheme and that all ranges of ability and social mix would be represented. Interestingly enough all the children of teachers at the school found themselves in the pilot group, including the head's child. Any parent who wished could withdraw their child from the pilot, none chose to do so.

The summer holidays saw various team members meeting to go out on field trips to work out the fine details ready for the new school year, frantic phone calls and lunches to hone the modules, and a lot of soul searching for what we were about to undertake. Everyone was ready!

St John's could never have known just how much the *Opening Minds* project would impinge not only on the Year 7 students but also throughout Key Stage 3 and then on through the school.

Homework

It wasn't long before it became clear that we had created a different type of learning which had resulted in a different type of student.

For example, the choice had been made to to avoid issuing a homework timetable. It wasn't even called homework! Part of the idea behind our learning strategy was the desire on the part of the students themselves to continue their learning after the end of the school day without the negative image in children's eyes that usually happens when the word 'homework' is mentioned. Ideally what was done in the classroom would be open-ended enough for them to want to continue or develop further, what they were doing in class, when they got home. In fact, homework was called something else that actually captures what we were trying to achieve 'work@home.fun'. It wasn't long before we realized just what had been unleashed!

Part of the confidence felt by the parents of the pilot students was that there were more frequent meetings held with them than is the norm, in order to keep them abreast of developments within the pilot. It was at one of these early meetings that they covered the hoary old chestnut of homework. School, it appeared was taking over their family social times! Their children didn't want to go out on visits and excursions; they wanted to concentrate on whatever project they were busy on with work@home.fun, furthermore, they did not approach their studies at home in the same way as their siblings who had been or still were at St John's; they were children who were eager to learn both inside and outside the school arena, they pushed themselves (and therefore their families) to the limit to do the best they could and beyond. Parents were excited but concerned. We were excited and, quite frankly, amazed!

This was something that they could be helped with. The teams met and discussed how to create less pressure at home. We didn't want a formal homework timetable but nor did we want to encroach on family leisure time either. The school opted therefore for an 'understood' timetable for the staff to follow. It was agreed what needed to be set and by whom and gave the tasks to the students with the proviso that they had to finish within a certain amount of time or when requested by their parents. They also needed to note for their own benefit just how much time they spent on a task. It was interesting that they often became very 'vague' when asked how long they had spent on something that had obviously been way over the time suggested!

During that first term, the pilot teaching teams were beginning to act in a strange way too. There were huddles in the corridors, staffroom, car park, wherever we crossed paths. Instead of casual chit chat, there was excitement about teaching strategies we had decided to experiment with; successful lessons that had been guided, not by the adult in the classroom but by the students themselves; disastrous lessons that had been laboured over in order to create what was felt had been a great idea, only to fail dismally. It seemed that every new week brought a problem that there was too little time to resolve but nevertheless a resolution needed to be found – yesterday. Looking back it is clear to see just how fired and inspired we were by the pilot. We were actually questioning and constantly revising the progress of our students. We weren't any longer simply imparting knowledge, we were actually questioning and constantly revising what we were doing, we were having weighty dialogues that were centred about learning to learn. There is no doubt that there were many low points. As dedicated teachers of course we always carried at the forefront of the pilot the notion that we could only justify it if it was seen to work better than traditional methods.

The search became more vigorous to find ways to complement learning in the classroom. Music was used to energize, excite or focus, Brain Gym® strategies were introduced to maximize the capacity of the youngsters to acquire new ideas and concepts. Those of us who were lucky enough to teach several lessons together chose at times to ignore the timetable. We worked through lunchtimes, brought sandwiches and had a picnic when the rest of the school were back in lessons. This was one area when classes really did enjoy not being the same as everyone else. While others were at lunch there was no sense of 'missing out', they loved the idea of having lunch when everyone else was hard at work. Nor were they distracted by the sound of fun and laughter as they worked through the lunch period. That *did* surprise me.

Despite the tiredness that was affecting all the staff towards the end of the first term, there was still a 'buzz' about what was trying to be achieved, and that 'buzz' was growing. It made us question what we had created and released; for the results of testing, internal and external evaluation and the many visitors that started to arrive on our doorstep all pointed towards the many differences they could see between the pilot group and what would have been expected from a traditional class of students. These differences were far more than had even been taken account of. I suppose our focus was so closely on the day-to-day delivery that it took others to point out the extent of the changes that were occurring, some of which are itemized on page 48.

Achievements of the pilot students

- The bonding of the students towards each other; they did whatever was needed to get the best from their classmates.

- The subtle change that occurred between the teacher and students, a partnership, founded on respect.

- Less able children were accorded respect and therefore did not feel disadvantaged.

- Less able students performed better and achieved greater success.

- The ethos that was encouraged allowed students to feel that it was OK to want to learn, studying was 'cool'.

- Boys' results matched that of the girls, and sometimes overtook them.

- Homework was seen as vital in order to complete work to the standard *they* wanted to achieve.

- Able students could fly ahead and deliver concepts that went far beyond Year 7 expectations.

- Students understood that learning did not only occur when they were in a formal, writing situation.

- Their oral skills improved enormously.

- Girls and boys mixed easily in any variety of groupings.

- Students did not have to have everything set out for them, given a challenge they were confident enough to cope within their pairs or groups.

- There was not a constant clamouring for the teacher, they were aware that they could help each other without the aid of an adult.

- Students were often amazed that a lesson had overrun, clock watching did not happen in these classes (teachers too were often caught out).

- Absences were less, students did not want to miss school.

- The medical room was rarely used, students did not want to let down their friends.

- Poor behaviour in the classroom was not a problem.

- These children did not need to be put 'On Report' for the entire year.

- The school counsellor noticed that these students did not require her help or intervention.

- They were able to sort out their own friendship problems.

- Their confidence almost caused other staff, outside of the pilot, to consider the students to be arrogant – the pilot teachers, however, applauded their initiative; it was a hard balance to work within.

- These students were always willing to help both teachers and the school and tended to throw themselves into all aspects of school life.

- The sheer joy of wanting to learn, knowing there were no barriers to hinder them.

- They appreciated that learning was fun!

Setting by ability

During the autumn term teams were busy on the next set of modules they needed to prepare. Meetings were often held to look at:

- the new modules

- the students

- organization of parents' evenings

- consideration of the reporting system to be created

- assessment of the students for:

  ➤ the competences

  ➤ subject knowledge.

It was quite clear that the progress made by all students was beyond what might have been expected from a traditional approach. The baseline data showed a significantly higher engagement with learning compared with the control group. However, it came as quite a shock to all of us when the head decided that if progress was to be maintained by all the teaching groups that had been created in September, the present groups had outgrown their usefulness. The less able had forged ahead and were doing far better than one might have hoped at this stage. The high achievers were performing at an amazing (almost scary) level and the students that would normally have been the backbone of the classes had also been pushed to greater success. The gap between all ability areas, although better overall for everyone, was causing a real schism. We didn't want to be reduced to pitching lessons towards the centre, the whole idea behind the success of the pilot was to always expect the best from the students. To allow the children to progress appropriately and in a way that extended them to the full, a new strategy was required.

This was a difficult time. The head had delivered his opinion, the teaching teams all disagreed, and the smell of mutiny was in the air! We debated at great length, after all, the classes had been sensitively fine tuned and they now knew each other very well, their strengths and weaknesses. They had been on a residential course with their classmates early in the autumn term and this had further built the strong bonds that were vital to the team spirit each class radiated. Certainly from the point of view of some subject areas, where large gaps had opened up, it was important that a reshuffle should take place as the next module was about to begin. However, most of us heard this pronouncement with a real sense of dread. What would happen to the team building, that delicate balance of friendships that had developed? We had worked hard to instil a sense of closeness, respect and understanding, each of the three classes were quite different and unique and here we were, about to throw them all up in the air and start again!

With a real sense of loss and sadness we went about the creation of three teaching groups that would be set according to ability. But...hadn't we just spent all of our time saying that the competences would drive the curriculum, not the subject? The only saving grace was that the classes would remain the same for their tutor group sessions, still with the same tutor. For all lessons, however, they would be in an upper, middle or lower teaching group.

What had originally been considered would be a difficult task, reconciling a student to a class based on their ability in *all* subjects, was, in fact, fairly easy. A few of us worked out where we thought each child was best suited to be placed. It is interesting to note that we knew the students so well that when the listings were shown to all teachers there was no need to change anyone around.

Grudgingly we had, with poor grace, done as the head had directed. However, as the year proceeded and the children continued to make dramatic progress it became quite clear that he had made the right decision. It was another reminder of the need to continually be prepared to be flexible in order to meet the challenges that were faced during that first year. Harder to note, was the fact that the students themselves were able to recognize their ability level when they saw the class they had been allocated, but again, the new curriculum came into its own. The confidence the students felt by working within the competences had given them the self-respect to appreciate that they had been moved into a class that was more in tune with the way they would learn, they could understand that they hadn't been 'demoted' or 'put down'. Yes, there were tears from a few students who felt that they couldn't cope with being separated from their friends, but once again, the realization that they required a different approach to their learning allowed them to successfully adjust to the moves. It was clear to them all that the classes were based on academic merit and mutual respect, and did not allow students to look 'up' or 'down' on each other.

Even thinking what the new classes were to be called took a long time. We couldn't call them by the usual letters we would use for tutor groups as they would now be teaching groups outside of the usual tutor system everyone was familiar with. We finally named them after the hills that surround the town of Marlborough and offer the only routes up and out of the town: Salisbury, Kingsbury and Granham. When they left Key Stage 3 the class names would disappear with them, it was a transitory step only.

Formal assessment

Our journey along the Integrated Curriculum route continued through into the summer term. The new classes followed the second modules, continuing to use the carousel system, with the teams adapting their teaching styles to accommodate the different needs of the newly created classes. Already there were discussions about what would be offered to the three pilot classes in Year 8 and what the implications were for the new intake of Year 7 in September. We had continued to find that the new curriculum was stretching the students and delivering the hoped for results. However, in May, the staff were informed that, contrary to anything that had ever been debated concerning assessment (which had been on-going) the pilot groups would be examined formally so that their progress could be measured alongside the development of the control group.

This again provoked protest! After all, we had spent the whole year stretching students to their limit, assessing them within the project and meeting any numbers of visitors who wanted to see what we had done. Students had been taught in a different style, using alternative benchmarks and acquiring different areas of knowledge. They had also been told that as they had been so carefully scrutinized there would be no need to follow an examination timetable for a week as the rest of the Year 7s always did. Needless to say, there were many unhappy students, parents and teachers, particularly given that the students would need to revise and take the examinations in a very short space of time and that they would spend whole days, with little respite between, sitting tests. The tests were a shock, unexpected, there was no time to revise steadily, and the three classes were working under enormous pressure. There was a real concern that their results could be affected by the 'pressure cooker' atmosphere they suddenly found themselves in.

How do you test an Integrated Curriculum child so that all aspects of their learning can be covered? Of course, there were different types of tests within the more traditional format of the Optional Tests, including a paper on problem solving. Interestingly, whatever pressure they were put under in the short term the results they achieved fully vindicated this new approach to learning. The outline of the test results are given opposite. We were little short of amazed!

Year 7 (First Cohort) Optional National Test Results			
English	% improving one or more levels	% achieving lower than KS2 result	% achieving two levels higher than KS2 results
Control group	42	4	0.75
Pilot group	54	1	11.4

Mathematics	Average KS2 results	Average level achieved in Year 7 Optional National Test	Overall gain
Control group	3.92	5.08	1.13
Pilot group	4.01	5.61	1.6

Science	Cells and variations %	Particles %	Reproduction %
Control group	49	48	51
Pilot group	64	62	70

The school was delighted with the success of the new project; however, that led to further sensitive problems that needed to be addressed. At the beginning of Year 7 all parents were supportive of the school, whatever group their child had been placed in. Parents whose children were involved in the *Opening Minds* pilot had obviously been kept in touch with the project as the year had unfolded, and informed of our successes. News of any type travels fast and a school is no different from anywhere else. The parents of the control group soon heard how well the pilot group were doing and, naturally, became quite strident in wanting their children to have the same opportunities. This is the way of all change of course, they would not have wanted to know if we had not outdone even our own modest expectations, so I suppose we must look upon it as a problem we were only too happy to have to take on board... Throughout the time the Integrated Curriculum has been running we have gone to great lengths to ensure that all students in the control group have received as good an education at St John's as they could get: such additional input has been ongoing as the students have moved through the Key Stage. As Dr Hazlewood had originally stated, no student was to be disadvantaged whatever the outcome.

As the year moved on the decision was taken to continue with the Integrated Curriculum, including all Year 7s in the next intake. With this announcement came the realization that what had started out as an experiment was definitely here to stay, and no one could afford to hide their head in the sand any longer. Furthermore, the way some of the pilot students had forged ahead with their learning would mean that there were imminent decisions to make regarding the availability of accelerated courses for them that would begin at Key Stage 3. Suddenly the stakes were much higher. There were obviously some subject areas that would accept the challenge of GCSE studies being made available at Key Stage 3; others, however able the students concerned, would be able to recommend that a move in that direction would be of no benefit whatsoever.

What has happened in subsequent years is that some subject areas have accelerated the pilot students to start their GCSEs in Year 9, others have chosen to take the time within the Key Stage to broaden and enrich further subject related skills and areas of knowledge. In 2004 the pilot group sat the SATs tests. The results are given below.

SATs test results			
		Level %	
		5+	6+
Science	Control	77	44
	Pilot	82	51
	Difference	+5%	+7%
Maths	Control	79	66
	Pilot	75	58
	Difference	-4%	-7%
English	Control	79	38
	Pilot	82	42
	Difference	+4%	+4%

It is difficult statistically to draw firm conclusions from this data. No child was disadvantaged academically by their involvement with the pilot. In English and science, however, which went well beyond the boundaries of the Year7/8 curriculum from the beginning, the results are more impressive. In terms of maths there are other factors that have contributed to this picture. Our internal data would suggest that there is actually no difference between control and pilot group performance. However, I leap ahead.

Second year (2002/2003)

At the end of the first year of the three Integrated Curriculum classes, the problem remained of how best to move their learning forward in Year 8. We were keen to let the students' learning be guided by all the subject specialists that were available to them. However, we still wanted to keep a sense of the storyline running through the new modules that were to be created for Year 8.

The creation of teams of teachers for the three pilot classes of the Integrated Curriculum in Year 8 was based on the establishment of four subject Schools (see opposite), where it was possible for them to create six-week modules of work for their subjects that could be effectively bound together by a common theme. The four subject Schools fell into this pattern:

Arts School	art, drama, music, PE
Humanities School	Classics, geography, history, RE
Languages School	English, French, German, Latin
Technology School	DT, ICT, mathematics, science

However, all was not plain sailing. The need to divide classes into four groups when doing DT (a health and safety requirement) meant they had felt unable to work within six-week modules. It had been thought that for Year 8 directorates should have their own autonomy in the delivery of the module even though they had to work within a common title. DT chose to work to a nine-week module length. However, what appeared to be a simple choice actually had huge ramifications for the School of Technology because as the modules unfolded DT drifted further and further out of step with their School. Yet again, the problem arose because those new to the Integrated Curriculum could not have been expected to fully understand the delicate balance that needed to be built upon by those in each School. They could not see the symbiotic relationship that was required to make the curriculum work successfully; this was a sensitive issue. We had wanted to draw directors and teachers who had not been part of the pilot scheme into our 'curriculum for the 21st century'; in doing so we had failed to realize that as they had not gone through the steep learning curve that the original teams had done, they were unaware of the finer points that made the new curriculum work.

With the creation of the four Schools of subjects there were now no longer six modules to follow throughout the year but 24! There was a real sense of students losing what theme they were following within what subject they were studying. Therefore a natural shift happened in Year 8. The subjects worked together within their separate Schools, which led to four curriculum areas being studied in the course of one week's lessons – so the sense of a common path was slowly being crushed by the different demands of the four Schools. This fragmentation was recognized as the third year rolled around and was addressed as we moved into the fourth year.

We were additionally stymied by the enormous amount of further professional development that was needed in order to distil to all what looked like minor changes in teaching and learning that collectively led to the huge changes that had become the Integrated Curriculum. Whatever staff development days or twilight sessions that were organized were not enough. With only one evening available each week for meetings after school there was too little time to catch up on a year's accumulation of new initiatives. This was apart from the dialogue that was going on among teachers who had been timetabled to teach the Integrated Curriculum across what would now be all nine classes in the new cohort of Year 7. The second year of the pilot was going to be a bumpy ride.

When any new initiative is introduced to a school there is a driving need to ensure that all teachers understand the philosophy that underpins the new ideas. It was quite clear that as the first year unfolded there was the need to alter and tweak the curriculum in order to create the most useful learning pathways for all subjects. In the second year of the pilot, drama and PE were brought into the scheme; this now meant that all subjects were represented. Subject directors and subject teachers were particularly keen to create a common core that each subject would need to deliver during the course of the year. From a subject point of view this was vital if teachers were to feel confident that they could deliver the curriculum requirements at Key Stage 3. Such additional ingredients, as it were, then had to be woven into the storyline of each module.

It was at this point that the original name used for the pilot, the Integrated Curriculum, was changed to the Alternative Curriculum. The reason for this was that although it certainly did rely on the need for subjects to work together and at times for teachers to work 'outside the box', there was much more to it than that. To continue to call it the Integrated Curriculum when so many new facets had been introduced to the learning of our students, particularly within the use of the competences, was to do it a disservice; we had moved on a long way from the curriculum ideals and models of the 1970s and needed to distinguish it as such.

There were now nine journeys unfolding instead of just three, so it was even more important to make use of 'The Book' to record each lesson. Here again, there were problems which highlighted just how difficult it was for teachers to comprehend what was needed. The fault was not theirs, but it did lead to real feelings of inadequacy for some. We had to support our teachers if that 'critical mass' was to be found.

The nine new teaching teams had been taken off timetable to create their individual journey through their modules. This was vital, as each team's lessons would be in a different order throughout the week depending on the timetable of every individual involved. The end result would be the same coverage of subject skills allied with the competences but the journeys would all cover the curriculum by a slightly different route.

There was another problem to deal with. The assistant headteacher, who had been a major figure in the creation of the *Opening Minds* project, left at the end of the previous year for a promotion in another school. He had also been the person responsible for the creation of the school's timetable, and had been fully aware of the need to make the teaching teams small in order to allow the teachers to really know their students and to make communication between them that much easier. However, when the new timetables were issued it was clear that such vital information had not been clarified to the new person in charge of creating the new timetable. The teaching groups were far too big, this meant that from the very start of the second year there would be problems in communication between the teams, especially as many teachers were involved in more than one team and were unable to be in several places at once when teams met to discuss progress. This did little to aid communication within the teams.

It was interesting to see how the delivery of the Alternative Curriculum was received by the new members of staff who were now involved. We had gone from a selected group of 21 volunteers to a group of over 70. NQTs did not tend to find a problem with either the content or the delivery of the curriculum; old timers who had been teaching a long while were able to remember the joys of the freedom of teaching outside the constraints of the National Curriculum. The group of teachers who found it the hardest were those who had taught only within the National Curriculum. For some, the freedom to change what could be attempted at Key Stage 3 was too heady a concoction.

A lot was being expected from those staff who had been drafted in to deliver Year 7's curriculum. We had failed to realize that there were those who actually felt that what had been done was detrimental to their subject area. They had lost some of their power of influence over the timetable; they felt slighted and undermined. There were others who genuinely felt that this was not the right direction to move towards, the transition was happening too fast and some of the values that they felt underpinned their subjects would be lost.

However, the biggest concern undoubtedly covered the area of the new techniques that were to be employed in the classroom. Most appreciated the vision of Guy Claxton's Learning to Learn but: What was the point of multiple intelligences? How would they incorporate Brain Gym® exercises in a busy hour's lesson that barely gave them enough time to deliver their subject matter? If a traditional teacher had been used to working from textbooks, how were they feeling when told it was a good idea to play music in lessons; let students take control of their learning and move a planned lesson in another direction; to physically make movement and shared working a vital component of the lesson; and as for the competences...? For them the new curriculum would undermine the very style of teaching they had been doing for years; furthermore, it would undermine them. Were they to be considered inadequate just because they were caught up in this whirlwind of change? The new expectations must have filled them with dread – either that, or they would choose to continue in their old ways and thus disadvantage our students. What a dilemma to find themselves in. We had to address the problems of everyone, not a task that would ever be seen as satisfactory to all I'm afraid.

Picking up the competences themselves was probably the area where most disquiet could be focused. Teachers certainly found that this part of the new learning caused them the biggest headache. Each of the competences was divided into several strands, so not only did they need to choose a single competence, they also needed to focus on the specific strand within the chosen area. This had to be recorded in 'The Book' (see page 43) every lesson and throughout the module teachers were expected to test two strands within the competences. They could not afford to see this as a grey area, that they would slowly be able to take on board; they needed to understand it all from the start so that they could assess satisfactorily. Looking back it must have been awesome for teachers new to the project to get a 'feel' for what was expected of them. Older hands had had a year to get their heads around the concepts, no doubt we were seen by some as an inner circle who knew all the answers; nothing could be further from the truth! We might have been a year ahead of them but we were still trying to find the 'right' answers. The project was still in its infancy; there were many more changes still to come.

Each 'Book' that travelled to every lesson with the students had a copy of the competences pasted in the front. When I look at it now I can understand just why it put a real sense of fear (I use the word after careful thought) in the hearts of our staff. The original set of competences that we had worked to were, on reflection, a nightmare to make sense of from their point of view. We had got used to them over the initial year; for anyone coming fresh to them (remembering there were now 70-plus involved) it must have been like pushing some of them over the edge. The teachers at St John's, as in most schools, are incredibly hardworking and professional. It is clear that when faced with the many strands within the competence structure they had been given far too much detail to get stuck in to. The many meetings that took place were usually reduced to enquiries about the minute detail within the competence framework, so much so that it was becoming a vehicle to hang all anxieties on. Something had to be done to save the situation, and it did seem that all were doomed to competence overload!

In order to try to resolve this downward spiral and help us all move forward, I asked someone who was not involved at all with the Integrated Curriculum to take a look at the competences and re-write them in a way that made them accessible to us all, including the students themselves. This was done so well that immediately the new paperwork went into each Book, every teacher was given their own copies and we made sure that the students had it printed in the front of their personal planners. At last it seemed that we were all on the same wavelength.

As the teaching teams were bigger in the second year it was clear that there was another problem looming. We had chosen to keep the carousel moving every six weeks in order to limit the amount of new modules any teacher would have to become familiar with. However, that did mean that for many teachers they did not know their students very well before the class moved on to the next module and the teachers were faced with another class' names and faces and learning journeys to become familiar with. What had worked well in the intimacy of small teaching teams in the pilot year was failing in the second year. Teachers can hardly be expected to cope with a new curriculum, new teaching strategies, new classroom ethos, new student/teacher relationships and then the added frisson of fear of a new class of youngsters to become familiar with. Too much, too much!

Third year (2003/2004)

This could not be changed in the second year but was immediately addressed as the third year unfolded. In order to make it easier, the two modules that were to be delivered by each team would now not be done at different points of the year, they would run back to back, so that the teachers would have a 12-week slot with each class. This certainly helped slow down the frenetic pace in getting to know their students as well as they needed to. However, other problems now arose. Also addressed in the third year was the size of the teaching teams. This was done by timetabling teachers who taught more lessons each week than they would normally, which then allowed them to cover other areas of the curriculum. For example, a humanities teacher would need to cover other subjects such as RE or Classics, as well as their own specialist subject of history. Some subjects such as the arts did not have enough specialist teachers to deliver the curriculum throughout the year, so it was necessary to teach some in only one 12-week block of the timetable. Therefore the situation arose that, in simplistic terms, a class would be submerged in art, or music, or drama for only one 12-week period throughout the whole year, and this too, of course, was not satisfactory. Again, there would also be problems when non-specialist teachers were expected to give a National Curriculum level for a subject that they were not wholly familiar with.

The fourth year and beyond

As we moved into the fourth year of the scheme, strategies were able to finally be put in place that covered the major problems encountered along the way. In practical terms it takes five years to embed new ideas into a school and oversee its development, we shall see...

- Every directorate has, over the past two years, refined and honed the curriculum that best serves their subject needs, the module content and, of course, the competences. They know what National Curriculum levels their students have attained and test and record them every 12 weeks. Meanwhile, every six weeks two competences are tested and recorded. It has been vital, of course, to ensure that not only the content of the module has been carefully mapped to be sure that all subject areas deemed necessary for the progress of the Year 7s has been covered but that all the competences (with their many strands) have been tested across the subjects when the pattern is looked at as a whole. The recording and subsequent use of such information has been a mammoth task and has required further strategic management moves to encompass it successfully.

- From September, there was no rotation of teaching groups. The class remain with one team of teachers who collectively map each individual student's progress.

- In order to give every subject specialist coverage in Year 7 it was necessary to increase, again, the size of the teaching teams. This was a point that was long discussed and appeared to deliver the only acceptable outcome.

- In the summer term 2004, visitors to school (Ofsted Inspectors), who left buzzing about what we had done to the curriculum, asked us why we called it the Alternative Curriculum they said: '...*it wasn't Alternative any more, it was* your *curriculum.*'

  Fair point! From September there is a full scheme of work for the Year 7s, that shows the development of the individual modules subject by subject and that shows the connection between each subject area. Never has such a comprehensive document been produced before and it is hoped that it will, for the first time, show the definitive progression of our students through their foundation year at St John's.

- Keeping the classes with one team of teachers will allow movement, if needed, between the classes. Beforehand this had been difficult and limited, as there was always the problem to face of whether the student being moved had covered the module work already. It had only been possible therefore for the child to move into two other classes. From September 2004 there was the choice of eight other classes that a student can go into, which gives much greater flexibility.

- Reporting will be far easier than previously. The teaching team seeing the students through the year collectively write the reports. That had not been possible when the classes rotated throughout the year. If they were only taught art in the first module, that teacher needed enough information to write a report on that child as well as those in the other two rotations that they had taken since. Remembering the individual students over many months having not having seen them was unsatisfactory to say the least! Also teams were drafted in to report on the child they were at present teaching. Sounds sensible, but it was not satisfactory. It meant that the Year 7 reports were written by teachers that had taken them for only a few weeks; core subjects would not have a problem but those teachers who saw their classes perhaps only once a week were at a disadvantage. They would need to check with the two other subject specialists that had taken them throughout the year, a cumbersome and time-consuming second-best solution. If you wanted to record the statistics and results of the child fine but the school wanted more than that, the essence and individuality of the child needed to shine through. After all, was not the premise behind the entire concept of putting the child at the centre?

- 'The Book' was still at the core of the journey through the modules. We've rejected hard-backed books, hard-backed files and soft plastic files in our search for the most efficient way to record the lessons. All have been discounted for various reasons; let's hope we've now hit on the best way to log the learning journey lesson by lesson and week by week.

- Competences are still seen as the vehicle to drive lessons forward. They are still what separates our teaching styles from the more traditional curriculum and so allow the students to acquire the skills they will need, to serve them through the many changes that no doubt will assail them through the 21st century.

- Changes at Key Stage 3 will impact considerably at Key Stages 4 and 5. Certainly there is now much that needs to be done in those Key Stages to carry through the natural progression of the skills based curriculum.

- Key Stage 3 is to be delivered in two years, not three. This is probably the biggest change that the implementation of the Integrated Curriculum has brought about. From a subject point of view, the tightening up of the areas deemed important for them to include for study at Key Stage 3 has allowed greater flexibility within the Key Stage. This now means:

1. In Year 7 we have the foundation year based on understanding and developing the competences in a module designed curriculum.

2. In Year 8 the focus will be on the curriculum, demands of the individual subjects, while continuing with the competences as the underlying structure. Therefore the Schools of subjects (see page 53) are no longer required; subjects will stand alone in Year 8.

3. In Year 9 students in the core subjects will sit their SATs (we see no need to move these into Year 8). The final year of Key Stage 3 will be seen as a time to begin GCSEs or else concentrate on broadening or enriching the learning of students within the individual subject areas.

So this new approach to learning has evolved, kicking and screaming. It has literally created a climate where hard-pressed teachers have needed to take time out to examine the very tenets that they have always accepted, the tenets that are based around a style of learning that is divided into subject areas.

It hasn't been easy and it hasn't been comfortable. Constraints of time and timetabling, individuals' demands and student needs have pulled in contradictory directions. There has been a delicate path to tread and yet, at the end of the day, decisions needed to be made that could never suit the requirements of everyone. However, steel is tempered by fire. In our new curriculum we have chosen to make a change for the better, to refuse to accept that what has always been is the right way forward. As Aristotle remarked:

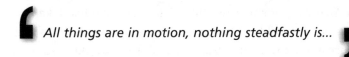

All things are in motion, nothing steadfastly is...

Therefore to focus on the changing demands of society and adapt and create a curriculum that would best reflect its needs for the future is what we have set out to achieve. Now, if we have got the balance right, all we need is to

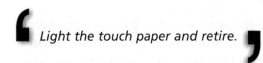

Light the touch paper and retire.

The rest lies with our empowered and enthusiastic students!

Chapter 4

The teachers' tale

Richard Smith and Lesley Spencer

This chapter is written by teachers of the Integrated Curriculum for those who will go on to practise much of what we say in their own classrooms. Our aims here are simple: to give an honest account of our experiences of teaching the Curriculum. It is our hope that in detailing the journey we have undertaken we will both inform and enlighten other classroom practitioners, while also encouraging them to experiment with this curriculum for the 21st century for themselves; the road from teaching the National Curriculum to facilitating the Integrated Curriculum can appear to be long and daunting but the adventure is, ultimately, both exhilarating and satisfying.

Although we initially trained as English teachers, in the course of writing this chapter we wished to gain an overview of opinion, one which reflected all the teaching staff across the school. With this in mind we approached and interviewed a wide range of staff from across the spectrum of academic disciplines, levels of management and responsibility, and teaching experience. We sincerely thank all of our colleagues for the following accounts, anecdotes and views, and the humour, honesty and candour with which they were offered.

Where will our journey take us?

For many of us our initial preconceptions about the Integrated Curriculum remain clear in our minds. Even now that we all have extensive experience of teaching the curriculum and are able to distinguish between myth and reality, these early preconceptions and – in many cases – mistaken beliefs provide an interesting indicator of how far we have all come in such a relatively short time. From our privileged retrospective stance we can light-heartedly dismiss the fact that, despite attending briefings which informed us and meetings which confused us, we were still varyingly unclear as to what was expected of us: from those who understood the principles of the Curriculum but were unsure how to apply them (*'I didn't really grasp that we were teaching competences; I understood that it was student-centred but I didn't know how to implement the skills.'*) to those who openly admit *'I didn't know what on earth it was all about!'*

Early on our diverse misconceptions fuelled much debate and reluctance to fully embrace the Curriculum. We understood that to deliver a skills based programme of study we had to actively move away from delivering our own subjects; thus many of us believed (and began to hear on the grapevine) that we could be going into the classroom to teach an art lesson and could in fact (accidentally) end up delivering a maths lesson! Indeed at the very beginning of our journey a number of our colleagues enthused that they were going into the classroom but were soon *'ripping up lesson plans'* because the students had very clear ideas of their own as to what they wanted to do. This prospect, naturally, did not inspire confidence in us all (*'I felt a little out of my depth'*), since some of us were *'a bit scared by the idea of teaching outside of my subject area'*. This issue also gave rise to some very real concerns that *'we appeared to be taking people away from subject specialism'* but such views also acknowledge that *'there are teachers out there who can make the teaching of others' subjects as adventurous and exciting as the teaching of their own'*.

Furthermore, it appeared that in linking our subjects together into a topic based module we were creating an artificial learning experience (*'Putting the story together was difficult... you were so used to being a science teacher, that taking account of what other subjects do, it felt like making your lessons fit; that was what it felt like to start with.'*). For some subjects it appeared that they were faced with the dilemma of breaking away from an already successful formula:

> *'Some subjects teach a set of basic skills and build from there; with others it's hard to choose which areas we're going to miss out. The pupils could be losing cultural enrichment and diversity.'*

Principally these comments reflect how we once viewed the Integrated Curriculum, how we felt before we overcame our initial fears and could begin to comprehend what was required of us: *'I felt inadequate... I didn't feel that everyone was on board; a lot of staff felt like they were on the outside looking in. But that was then; it has changed.'*

Once the initial pilot group had experienced the first year of the Curriculum, these pale preconceptions were soon replaced by vivid positive teaching experiences. One teacher proudly comments: *'A huge number of staff who are non-subject specialist have come to me and said, "This has been my favourite thing I've taught this year".'* And so word spread among many of us that teaching the Curriculum *'would be a positive experience; that the children would be more confident and enthusiastic and motivated'* and soon we found *'that's exactly what they were!'*. Our fears were firmly allayed. One colleague comments:

> *'I taught both students who were experiencing the Integrated Curriculum and the traditional Curriculum and found that there was a big difference. All three of the pilot groups within the Curriculum were noticeably more enthusiastic. To start I felt a little out of my depth... but I didn't need to: it's a team-effort. I wasn't there to keep asking them questions and give them information. They [the children] start group and class discussions, where some who have more knowledge speak up and lead the discussion. I was able to sit back and facilitate.'*

Why have we chosen this route?

As a teaching body our starting point for making the transition from the traditional Curriculum to the Integrated Curriculum was to develop our own understanding of the principles which underpin the programme. Moreover, as individuals we also needed to decide to what extent we agreed with this philosophy, and to determine how far this would impact upon our personal teaching pedagogy:

Higher, Faster, Stronger Module: investigating heart rate

'Over the past three years we've been learning a new way of teaching. I used to do creative things in my lessons before the Alternative Curriculum but, in terms of understanding how the students are thinking, I don't believe we've really ever grasped it before.'

For the teaching staff this has perhaps been one of the most interesting facets of the Curriculum's evolution: although the corps views may have differed as to the initial impact upon various departments *('From our point of view we had already spent many years moving away from the image of being a subject which is textbook based towards a proactive, skills based learning environment. I felt that for us this was almost a step back, a retrograde move')*, the overwhelming consensus opinion is that a skills based approach to teaching is advantageous for many reasons.

From the teachers' perspective it has allowed many subject areas to review and redress their programme of study for Years 7 and 8, those year groups which could traditionally suffer from featuring low on our list of priorities. It has guaranteed that we adopt a more coherent and consistent approach to our classroom delivery *('It has encouraged all directorates to work at the same level: to promote group-work, leadership skills, lateral thinking; to integrate numeracy, literacy, music, art, history, all into the same lessons')*, while employing creativity to ensure that our lessons never become formulaic *('It encourages teachers away from simply placing a textbook in front of the students')* and continue to appeal to a wide range of learning styles:

'In the past certain subjects may have been viewed as being a little boring; they needed something radical like this to shake them up. But now all subjects work hard to make them exciting and fun.'

From the students' perspective we have found the Curriculum promotes a clearer structure for developing conceptualized thinking; for those who were previously unable to identify *'the links between practical and theoretical learning [the Curriculum] helps them to grasp the ideas which underpin what they are trying to do'*. Lateral thinking is actively encouraged through skills transference: *'it shows them that skills are interchangeable, partly because the teachers themselves have been interchangeable'*. Again and again colleagues comment on the heightened levels of *'enthusiasm', 'independence'* and *'maturity'* which skills based learning fosters within the classroom:

> *'The hardest element to adapt was to put the onus even more upon the students. But you just have to step back and see what they come up with; let them have more power within the classroom. It's worked. They come in and expect to run themselves, they get themselves into groups, they're organized. It makes them more mature compared to the normal Year 7.'*

St John's Lower School

Primarily, this should be attributed to our heightened expectations of even the very youngest students, which this Curriculum delivers to them. It is common practice, and a requisite feature of developing problem-solving skills, to pass responsibility for planning tasks, group management and delivering the plenary (to mention but a few) back over to the students. Our empowering of our students, our resolve *'to let the students take more emphasis for their own learning...for them not to have preconceptions when they go into a lesson'* now means that students are able to carve their own learning pathways which can be tailored to suit individual learning needs; it is this sense of learning relevance which is pertinent to each individual student that allows them to invest both academically and emotionally within the classroom:

> *'[Students] feel more confident within the classroom because they have been given more choice.'*

'Students can now have more confidence to explore those areas of learning which interest them. Why should we be saying that "you have to learn X, Y and Z"; that can make [students] hate some subjects because they're not getting the information they need or want. It's really important that the students learn what they want to learn; we need to help them find their paths for later on in life.

The feedback from our colleagues on the second year of implementation was equally interesting. Over 70 staff were involved at this time and INSET was provided to integrate new staff to the methods and goals of what was now called the Integrated Curriculum. After INSET a questionnaire was distributed in order to assess teachers' understanding of the Integrated Curriculum. We have left this in the form of the original responses (see pages 63–66) to help the reader understand what it felt like for these 'new' teachers on their learning journey.

Responses from the teacher questionnaire on the Integrated Curriculum from September 2002

1. In your own words what are the aims of the Integrated Curriculum?

   - Direct students to develop skills which they can then apply in a variety of subject based areas.

   - To encourage students to become independent learners and to nurture a desire to learn.

   - To give pupils skills and experiences which will enable them to love learning and carry on doing it confidently all through their lives.

   - To give pupils responsibility for their own learning and encourage the use of new learning and teaching styles.

   - For learning to be a continuous curve for students; for their learning to be self-motivated and less directed; to offer various learning styles to every student.

   - To promote and motivate the self-learner and to enthuse and excite through cross-curricular lessons.

2. How have you set about achieving those aims in your lessons?

   - Being aware of my own teaching and learning style preferences and broadening teaching techniques; also by being aware of individual needs and catering to this.

   - Deliberately stepping back and presenting a task for which the students have then had to organize themselves.

   - By shifting the responsibility towards students for their learning; being a facilitator rather than a didactic teacher.

   - Showing *how* students can learn rather than *what* to learn – giving a task that needs to be achieved by the end of the lesson.

   - Ensure that various teaching and learning styles are on offer – changed ways that topics are approached and asked children to devise ways to acquire vocabulary.

   - By being more confident about letting them lead and by using a variety of teaching and learning styles.

3. Have you needed to develop specific skills in order to teach within this pilot?

   - No.

   - No, but I have had to think ahead.

   - I have needed to develop confidence that students can take on responsibility.

   - I have to be more open minded and relaxed.

   - I am learning more emotional literacy skills.

   - I use some of the multiple intelligences that I hadn't thought of before.

4. What issues have been most difficult?

   - Time.

   - Working out how one lesson a week can be meaningfully utilized within an integrated context.

   - Lack of time to catch up with other staff on same module; occasional lack of expertise when following on from a teacher working from a totally different discipline.

   - Not enough support on using or developing multiple intelligences.

   - Finding the balance between giving the students information and allowing them time to find out more for themselves.

   - Letting go.

5. What support have you been given that has been most helpful

   - Handouts.

   - Twilights.

   - Time, meetings – team-building time.

   - Guidance and someone to talk to.

   - Support of other teachers on the scheme.

   - Dialogue with colleagues.

6. Have you created any of your own support systems either for your own benefit or for that of staff?

   - Yes.

   - Asking specific questions to staff involved last year and convince myself that it is acceptable to not always know.

   - Informally with phone calls to others.

   - As team leader I get the problems first and go to those above me.

   - Planning with others.

7. How do your lessons differ from other lessons you teach beyond the pilot?

   - I don't always follow the National Literacy Strategy.

   - Structure.

   - I do less talking – pupils are more involved.

   - More exciting – know the pupils more and behaviour.

   - Less prescriptive and less content driven – use of different learning styles.

8. How have children responded to your approaches?

   - Positive, enthusiastic learners – keen to participate and interact.

9. What is the working atmosphere in lessons?

   - Lively, congenial, enthusiastic, keen to learn.

10. Can you describe the teacher/student relationship?

    - Friendly, less distant than with other groups; aim for partnership approach – push some, praise others; students confident but know boundaries.

11. Differ from other classes?

    - No; more student/teacher interaction which is less formal and more task oriented.

12. Does discipline differ?

    - More group-work and mutual working through issues, students become less disinterested and unmotivated.

13. How are you monitoring the skills development?

    - Through discussions with students and staff – evaluations after lessons.

14. What difficulties are you experiencing in the development of these skills?

    - Assessing at the end of six weeks is challenging and new; finding opportunities to try everything is difficult.

15. Are you aware of what other groups are doing and how that work impinges on the subject area you are representing?

    - Mostly through 'snapshot' conversations – more so when with regard to 'usual' subject area.

16. How do you feed back to directorate?

    - Originally, material is available to directorate, follow-up feedback is via line managers via checklist and verbally.

17. What is their response?

- Varied – some are happy, others are concerned that national strategy is not being covered as it ought to be.

18. What other support would you like?

- Time – with colleagues.

19. What are the most positive outcomes from the pilot?

- Improved student self-esteem; reassessing role of teacher in relation to aims; seeing the whole child develop; enjoyable atmosphere of the lesson.

The second year was more challenging than the first in many ways; the programme was rolled out to the entire year, teams were bigger and the pace increased. Some teachers taught more than one band and were learning 60 new names every six–eight weeks; others taught both Year 7 and the pilot group. Those who were thoroughly immersed in the teaching found that they were transferring the skills and approaches to their traditional classes through the school.

Looking back – interviews with teachers

As we undertook this project of recording the teachers' tale, we asked teachers from across the curriculum range for their comments.

The director of English felt that good English teachers were already engaging in the types of interactive, emotionally intelligent teaching that were encouraged by the Integrated Curriculum. She was in favour of the philosophy behind the programme and applauded the focus on Year 7 as a transition year. The assessing of skills required by the competences, to a great degree, was already a part of English through the Key Stage 3 National Strategy. The knowledge of one's students improved once the idea of rotations was muted. Team meetings so that links could be built were more valuable than whole-school presentations. The best way forward would be to establish a core of teachers who would embed the skills and values and who develop a team-oriented approach. More training for new staff was also mentioned as a need. Team teaching in a block of time could be trialled whereby, for example, an English teacher and a science teacher could teach science based report writing as part of a science experiment in such a manner that would give a 'real life', meaningful context for the report.

The head of the religious education department was well aware of the tensions between the mandates of the LEA's religious education programme, known as the Agreed Syllabus, and the Integrated Curriculum. During the pilot, one of the humanities teachers, also an RE teacher, ensured that RE was a part of the pilot, in terms of teaching sensitivities and deeper understanding of religious concepts.

As the programme continued, with Year 8 being taught in 'schools' (see page 52) RE specialists were a part of each band. However, when the programme was rolled out to all Year 7 classes, it became apparent that not every group had an RE teacher in every rotation, a worry for this head of department. The solution was to support other humanities teachers who suddenly found themselves in the position of having to deliver all of RE input per week to Year 7 students, even though RE was not their specialist area. Schemes of work which had existed pre-Integrated Curriculum were adapted to fit within the 'story' for each module.

In the third year, with the head of RE's imminent departure to New Zealand, the decision was made to design schemes of work that complied with the Agreed Syllabus and made more of 'a nod' to the Integrated Curriculum storyline, leaving teachers to deliver the skills in such a way that the purposes of both would be well served. An interesting benefit to the RE department was that the assessment for learning strands in the Key Stage 3 National Strategy had already been embedded in the schemes of work that had been adapted to suit the Integrated Curriculum, three years earlier than needed. In a roundabout way, the philosophies of the teaching of skills had been met by this department, even though some of the directorate originally wanted the Integrated Curriculum to go away, leaving teachers to be teachers of RE – a subject that can be 'patchy' in terms of coverage at KS2. Thinking about process, thinking about thinking were laudable and achievable. The best 'bits' of the Integrated Curriculum (and the Key Stage 3 National Strategy), the skills and processes, could be applied at KS4 and KS5 to enhance learning. Individual lessons were much more exciting and rewarding, though the challenge of 'fitting square-head pegs in round holes' was challenging. Assessment for learning in terms of the competence of 'learning to learn' was rewarding and positive. In the future, focus on the skills based development, learning attitudes and assessments that take into account process would be this teacher's preferred way forward. Assessment needs to be consistent and meaningful; with a degree of depth and importance.

Higher, Faster, Stronger Module: students investigate heart rate

Another member of staff felt that directors had not been fully involved at the planning stage and that a number of preparations were happening 'behind closed doors'. The philosophy of bettering the 'client's' experience was laudable but this particular member of staff felt that he was kept in the dark about the delivery of the building blocks that underpinned the programme. This member of staff became more involved in the second year of the programme and taught the pilot group. He found that traditional expectations of discipline were lacking but that at the end of the second year the higher and lower Integrated Curriculum groups were more creative than the 'control groups'.

The basis of the Integrated Curriculum was found to be similar to the Key Stage 3 National Strategy. The biggest advantage of the programme, from this staff member's point of view, was that the project acted as a 'catalyst to make teachers look at the way we teach' and has had positive knock-on effects throughout the school, a comment echoed by other members of staff. Students have become more involved in their learning and are more active participants in the process, though at least one member of staff felt that this was more successful with the higher ability sets.

In terms of assessment, one member of staff was worried that his directorate has lost the ability to gain an impression of levels of achievement or attainment early on in KS3 because his subject was sometimes taught by non-specialists and that his subject specific concepts and skills had been diluted and/or not properly assessed. This issue was dealt with in the second year of the programme with more of the directorate teaching their subject specialist areas in Year 7 and by introducing a subject specific baseline assessment in Year 7 which also assessed the Integrated Curriculum skills. This member of staff was able to address any deficiencies by teaching the pilot group.

NQTs were an integral part of the programme, indeed several formed part of the core teachers for the pilot group. It was very clear to one of the NQTs that they were responsible for the teaching of skills, using their subject based content. The difficulty was that there never seemed to be enough time to prepare responses to the developing storyline. One memorable lesson occurred with the lower group who surprised the teacher by suggesting an alternative approach to the planned, differentiated method; the alternative approach was successful. This teacher enjoyed the rotations of students every six to eight weeks and found that rather than repeating the content in the same manner, that she, by natural progression of the story, varied the content and the assessment for each of the three groups she saw. Here, too, the feeling was that the skills taught were more valuable than rigidly sticking to the storyline. This NQT was more comfortable with the second and third rotations of the programme where she was teaching skills within the subject area of her expertise.

The reporting and assessing procedure, with what seemed like countless OMR sheets, was sometimes seen as a necessary evil – some teachers found that The Book (the log book), carried by the pupils in Year 7, while a good idea, was better managed in the first year.

Several lessons were exciting; while reading *Pig-Heart Boy* by Malorie Blackman, co-ordination with a biology teacher, preparation of an understanding of the heart's structures and functions with diagrams and discussion, culminated with an 'English' lesson focusing on dissecting a heart and comparing the process to that described in the text. Lessons occurred where the focus was on skill development and re-creating a 'real' world experience of poverty with the 'haves' versus the 'have-nots' with the teacher acting as a 'bank', while some students needing to barter and trade their 'goods' for scissors or other tools of the trade tested students' abilities to 'think outside the box', and form alliances and trading blocks to accomplish the goals.

Physical education (PE) was initially outside the pilot programme and its director was a bit hesitant about the potential dilution of the teaching of sport; while teaching sport and physical education in the context of 'Higher, Faster, Stronger' was 'exciting', how one taught sport in the context of 'Forests' was a bit of a mystery. The PE curriculum therefore remained largely similar to that taught in most schools. During the second year of the programme, with the focus being on the development of the competences, PE became much more involved with the programme. Rotations in PE groups in the first year did not always mesh with the modular rotations in the

Integrated Curriculum, either in terms of time or in terms of the composition of the teaching groups. The third year was the most productive: PE teaching groups rotated in step with DT rotations; assessments in line with the competences which were sport-based were developed and implemented; and timetabling was eased, so that four teachers taught three tutor groups and could stream them according to talent, ability and interest.

The directorate facing perhaps the greatest challenges in terms of integrating content, storyline and skill was MFL, which ended up teaching not only French, but also German to each group, each fortnight. Traditionally, one band would be taught a language, while another band was taught another. The teacher in charge of KS3 was given the responsibility of developing the MFL content. At the onset, MFL had not yet adopted the Key Stage 3 National Strategy, though the directorate was aware of and already implementing a skills based programme. The first year, working with a very small group of teachers was fantastic – planning was a group activity and all teachers knew what each other was covering. Knowing what was happening in what was traditionally an 'English' lesson was novel and interesting. A non-specialist (a trained scientist) ended up teaching German to one group which had the knock-on effect of offering two languages to the entire year group as the programme rolled out to the full year, with the exception of two targeted groups, each of whom was introduced to only one language. Working in a cross-curricular manner was the highlight of the first year. Being aware of the competences and working with the multiple intelligences had knock-on benefits at KS4.

There was some concern that students in the pilot group who were offered two languages would be behind when they merged with their 'control group' counterparts, but in the third year it was found that the group did catch up quite quickly, perhaps as a result of being 'taught differently'.

As the Integrated Curriculum progressed, MFL lessons that were offered were changed so that three MFL language lessons were offered a week. In year three of the programme, the first full set of students chose a main language, either French or German, and a second choice of Classics, Latin or the other MFL. In 2004 the programme changed again so that Year 7 students are offered two lessons a week in each of German and French, taught by different teachers. We are fortunate that every MFL teacher can offer both German and French at KS3.

Assessment of the competences was integrated with the traditional MFL assessments of reading, writing, and speaking and listening. Statements from the competences were translated into student-friendly 'I can' statements, with focus on self- and peer assessments being implemented.

This teacher, too, felt that by implementing the Integrated Curriculum, we, as a school, were ahead of the curve in terms of the demands of the Key Stage 3 National Strategy, both in terms of teaching and learning, as well as assessment.

How far have we travelled?

With four years of teaching the Integrated Curriculum behind us, we have all worked extremely hard to adapt both our Schemes of Work and our mindsets, to adjust our planning, the focus of our lessons and even the vocabulary which we use within the classroom: we are now 'facilitators' and 'learning managers', and our 'pupils' are now 'students' to whom we impart 'competences', and for whom we no longer 'set homework' but recommend 'extended learning'. Yet, we have taken these changes in hand and risen to the challenge with which we were faced. And with the experience we have gained we can begin to recognize the wider implications and ramifications which the Curriculum has had.

For some directorates the advent of the Curriculum has had a far-reaching and radical effect upon their Key Stage 3 programme: *'It has been completely transformed. We have ditched all our old Schemes of Work and rewritten them to focus on the Integrated Curriculum.'* For others it has had a reassuring influence, confirming that the skills based approach which some directorates had already been developing was indeed successfully placing the student and their learning at the centre of the classroom experience:

> *'We were already a skills based department, so the principles of the Integrated Curriculum have been those which lie behind the teaching of a number of my colleagues for a number of years.'*

But the successful delivery of the Integrated Curriculum must go beyond shifting the focus of our teaching towards skills based learning, it is also deeply rooted within the topic-based approach which we have adopted. Through the uniform delivery of the six thematically linked modules (Being Unique; Higher, Faster, Stronger; Making the News; Going Places; Forests; and Counting the Cost), we are helping our Year 7 students to overcome the transition from primary to secondary school by presenting learning in a format with which they are already familiar; this contributes fundamentally to the confidence and empowerment which the students feel:

> *'I like how we can discuss what the students are doing in other lessons, I would never have done that before. It's really valuable. In the past students thought that if they hadn't been taught something they didn't know it but now they can make links between subjects. It's more like the primary school experience where students have a common thread, a common theme between subjects.'*

The Curriculum has meant that we can now monitor and assess levels of learning in ways that using National Curriculum levels could not previously encompass; we are more consistently adept at recognizing and building upon individual progress. Directorates have *'devised new systems for recording skills and tracking how well [students] are doing. Instead of giving them a traditional grade we can now track individual development.'* With this shift in perception now firmly embedded in our teaching philosophy we can also identify secondary effects outside of our Key Stage 3 teaching; in both Key Stages 4 and 5, we are handing over the responsibility for learning with increased confidence to our students:

> *'At GCSE and A-level we're teaching them to develop independence, so teaching it from Year 7 helps to reinforce this higher up in the school.'*

And although we have yet to see a year group which has followed the Integrated Curriculum progress through to Key Stage 5, we accept that *'the students now think differently'* irrespective of how far they have progressed through our programme.

It is important that we pause briefly for a moment to consider the impact of the Key Stage 3 National Strategy upon our delivery of the Integrated Curriculum. With the arrival of the Strategy in September 2001, the delivery of Key Stage 3 lessons was destined to change throughout schools nationwide. Here was a programme of teaching which, similar to our Curriculum, advocates a skills based, pupil-centred and personalized learning programme:

'It is based on four important principles:

- **Expectations:** establishing high expectations for all pupils and setting challenging targets for them to achieve;

- **Progression:** strengthening the transition from Key Stage 2 to Key Stage 3 and ensuring progression in teaching and learning across Key Stage 3;

- **Engagement:** promoting approaches to teaching and learning that engage and motivate pupils and demand their active participation;

- **Transformation:** strengthening teaching and learning through a programme of professional development and practical support.'

(Key Stage 3 National Strategy 2004)

Change was inevitable within our school and, indeed, all schools because of the Strategy, but we perceive our evolution as being *'more extreme, more effective and will go on to be even more successful because of the Integrated Curriculum'*. However, there are important differences between the two approaches since our Curriculum moves away from the confines of individual subjects, liberating the students from the boundaries of subject content in order to focus upon the fundamental learning principles which underpin our teaching:

> *'I think that what we're doing with the Integrated Curriculum is what the Key Stage 3 National Strategy is trying to achieve within individual subjects… we've just opened it up to teaching skills irrespective of subject.'*

Thus we are, once again, looking forwards, preparing our students for the future where transferable skills will be valued as highly as subject knowledge. From this perspective we can now say *'Once the Key Stage 3 strategy arrived we were able to say "Yes, we already do that"'* and therefore can conjecture *'that we've had a greater success at implementing the National Strategy because… we had already jumped in at the deep end and learned how to swim'*.

Where will the road lead us next?

Part of the joy of our journey has been encountering challenges and responding to them collectively in constructive and creative ways, progressing forwards together, both teachers, managers and students, so that we can all feel a sense of ownership and pride in the Integrated Curriculum as it currently stands: *'it's there, it's being done and the students are responding well. No big changes need to be made… we simply need to tweak small areas here and there.'* We do not wish to sacrifice creativity and originality and fun, for a fruitless search for perfection.

Our quest to create a curriculum for the 21st century has allowed us to appreciate that as teachers we should not disregard teaching practices of the past; *'we must not create something totally artificial; why fight against years of evolution?'*

Instead we must appreciate that we are now eager to experiment; we must employ tried, tested and successful teaching practices but approach them from new and exciting perspectives. However, in our search to refine and develop this programme we must also allow *'time [for it] to be embedded'* within the psyche of the whole-school community. Above all, we are united in our belief that:

> *'The future has to be the students; we have to forget our own needs as teachers, doing those things which we find easier. We have to do what's best for the students, give them a good start in life through their learning.'*

Therefore, should we be asked if we are prepared to undertake such a journey again? If we are prepared to have our preconceptions, our philosophies and pedagogy challenged? If we are prepared to search further and longer in order to support such a belief?, we shall always give a heartfelt and resounding 'Yes' and feel proud to be able to do so.

Going Places Module: exploring fabrics

Going Places Module: exploring fabrics from around the world

Chapter 5

The students' tale

Kathy Pollard

St John's was a school recognized for its caring role and its very high academic standard. We also placed a high emphasis on developing a proper set of values based upon respect, responsibility and pride in yourself and your environment. Despite this it was felt we could still improve upon the quality of the education we offered to our students.

With our new curriculum our primary aims were to:

- create independent and highly motivated learners;

- place learners in the driving seat;

- develop people who 'love learning so much, and also learn so well, that they will learn whatever needs to be learned';

- create a cohesive learning experience removing the barriers to effective learning.

Constance Kamil, a teacher and educational researcher, argued that the traditional educational experience was one in which many students are forced to accept schooling which creates academic failures, discipline problems and unemployable drop-outs. The Plowden Report (HMSO 1967) commended the practice of first-hand experience, play and avoidance of over-directed activity. We have built upon these approaches, encouraging students to have fun so they will learn more readily and be prepared for tasks that are more demanding. This is especially pertinent if set in a context of how to move forward via positive experiences and recognizable progress to meet agreed targets. It is through stimulating activities like this that students will be able to explore links and variations, identifying what is concrete and what is reversible or subject to change and as such within their control.

Students have reported back over and over again that they thrive on challenge and problem solving. As they mature intellectually they are able to engage in logical thought using symbolic and abstract concepts. This is the stage at which they have become autonomous learners and can contribute to their own and others' understanding of their world and its complexity.

As a well-respected school with an effective primary–secondary transition programme already in place we set about reviewing the curriculum experience from the students' perspective. Prior to introducing our new curriculum we had called our lower school entrants 'pupils', reflecting the fact that they were end-users in the process of teaching. Significantly we now refer to them as 'students' giving them an interactive role in their own education. This fundamental change reflected very clearly the move that was made to put them centre stage in all our thinking and planning.

To give an early idea of how successful we were, after three years some students actually said in a conference for visiting educationalists that they now saw their role as teaching the teachers how to teach them!

Induction – learning is fun

Our normal student experience would begin with visits from staff to our primary feeder schools and visits for Year 6 students for a variety of activities covering several curriculum areas. Induction consists of a two-day visit in June (see below) but for some students this would be extended depending on their needs. Induction programmes have changed considerably in line with our new skills based curriculum, and we have rewritten the approaches and activities to set our expectations that the students will learn to think for themselves and solve everyday problems by employing common sense rather than relying on others to sort things out for them. We have designed a range of activities which explore their ability to work in teams and to solve problems; these focus on the tutor group and settling into the school routines. The students also complete exercises designed to identify their multiple intelligences and their self-esteem levels. The second day is a fun day with a medieval storyline following a group of friends through a series of 'hands-on' challenges. They cross flooded rivers, defend a castle, pay taxes with goods and chattels, rescue an apothecary and generally have great fun. What they will take away with them is a clear message which shows what they can achieve and that learning is fun.

Induction Programme

Day 1

Getting to know you

The focus is to provide a relaxed and friendly environment where students can safely explore the skills they need to operate effectively within the tutor group. Use as much of the fun factor as possible. Some items are essential as they feed into other systems – these are printed in bold and must be completed.

Contents

1. Ice breakers and energizers.
2. Making new friends, what makes a good friend, signing certificates.
3. Targets for the day and Certificate for successful completion of tasks.
4. The school day, breaks and lunchtime arrangements.
5. My learning profile, highway code to learning, tutor group summary.
6. Multiple intelligences, tutor group summary.
7. Who are you?
8. Getting to know you – self-esteem summary.

9. St John's code of conduct, behaviour management in the classroom.
10. Know your school. Timetables. The treasure trail and maps.
11. Welcome booklet.
12. Simple problem solving.
13. School dress and PE kit and equipment.

Day 2

Medieval Marlborough

On this day the students will start with their tutor but will then experience some room and staff changes which they can expect in September. The theme for the day will be a medieval storyline where students will work in teams to complete a set of challenges (to the best of their ability!). The emphasis will be on developing the skills of relating to people, managing situations, learning and thinking. You do not need to know the answers or how to achieve them, that is for the students to discover!

There may be visits from the Young People's Support Service; they are going to begin observations of some students with a view to working with them from the start of the autumn term. To help us target students with needs, please record concerns on the sheet provided. We will then set up IEPs and IBPs (individual education plans and individual behaviour plans) for the start of term for students with unresolved issues.

Go through the teamwork pack to help them develop an understanding of the skills they need to develop. Organize the groups so that there is a mix of students, boys/girls and different schools in each group if possible. Watch that vulnerable or isolated students are not left to be picked last; you might use them as the starting point for groups.

Talking through the tasks reinforces the skill development and can be particularly useful in helping the less skilful student realize the steps that are needed for improvement. It is also a chance to explain some of the competence descriptors with the more able groups.

Throughout the day students will complete a set of linked challenges designed to tap into a variety of thinking skills and learning styles. Completion of all tasks is not essential – some can be done as a class activity or in small groups.

Development of effective learning habits

When they begin Year 7 in September a lot of tutorial time is spent learning about how to develop effective learning habits and understanding their own strengths and weaknesses. The students are made more familiar with their learning styles by the tutors helping them to translate what they have done in class into the jargon of learning. They will have the opportunity to find out what it means to have a high interpersonal score and how that can best be used; similarly they learn how they can improve areas where their skills are less well developed. It has been noticeable that once students are armed with this self-knowledge they begin to negotiate outcomes which suit their learning profile. This is not ability linked but is directly attributable to methods and approaches

Students share a love of learning

with which they have achieved success. They might for instance be able to produce a mind map rather than an essay or a storyboard instead of a rough draft; email a PowerPoint presentation; or do an oral report on a tape recorder.

At St John's we not only issue a breakdown of each student's multiple intelligence scores but also a tutor group summary which identifies the group's strengths and weaknesses. For instance one tutor group might have strengths in interpersonal and kinesthetic learning while another might have mathematical and intrapersonal strengths. While this is a generalization it offers a way for teachers to direct their early teaching and learning strategies to methods that give the best opportunity for initial success. Tasks can then be extended for individuals to develop areas in which they are less secure. If a student is not making sufficient progress or is causing concern then teachers look at the personal profile and negotiate alternative strategies which might enable the student to access the work more easily. Where a student has particular learning needs this strategy has been especially helpful because they tend not to feel quite so different when given the opportunity to record or work in a different way.

Students with learning difficulties or specific learning needs thrived on the approaches in this curriculum. Initially it was because the emphasis was on group skills and a lot of emotional intelligence work was covered; subsequently there were fewer problems with 'labels and stigma'. The experience of sharing activities with mixed ability students and the respect for each others' comments and contributions empowered the less able to feel confident in offering their thoughts and ideas in safety without fear of ridicule. There is no doubt that the weaker students gained significantly from this experience. Educationalists often promote mixed ability groupings to enable students to experience intellectual challenge when their literacy and numeracy abilities are not reflected in their ability to communicate in more academic ways. We have found that it goes beyond this and enables all students to see themselves as successful in many different spheres and not just in relation to higher academic scores.

The modules

In the initial year of the pilot students were taught by small teams of teachers in a six-week module. The modular storyline was developed by the team who focused upon the competences and integrated the curriculum content. The smaller team of teachers made transition easier and enabled teachers to get to know the students far better. The teams rotated so that each class was taught by three sets of teachers over the year. Some students found this stimulating and dynamic as each new module got off to an exciting start. Other students did find that getting used to new sets of teachers was unsettling. In the second year of the pilot we ran the modules back to back so teaching teams only changed twice. By the third year the staff training was sufficiently advanced and the competences embedded into the curriculum that we decided that staff would not rotate. This has the benefit of more stability for the students.

When the pilot year progressed to Year 8 we began by combining subjects into four broad bands, a continuation of this interlinking of experiences and knowledge. By this time we had become so aware of the success that we took steps to teach the same learning skills across the whole of Year 8 and into Year 9, so that those students who had not been in the initial Year 7 pilot were given the chance to develop the same learning skills. Many of their teachers also used the same approaches and skills across the whole year group. This minimized the gap that had arisen in the pace of learning.

The results – student involvement

No sooner had we started the integrated curriculum than people were asking us for results and data, visitors abounded and students became immersed in a broad range of activities which we could not have foreseen in a normal school.

> *'The Integrated Curriculum works well because it seems to make everything clearer than before.'*
>
> Year 7 student in an interview with the RSA evaluator, Barry Wyse, November 2001

'You have the chance to learn how to learn' – highlighting the way in which students are taught, more critically the quote continued *'At first I wasn't so sure about the whole module thing but as time went by it grew on me and I liked it more and more.'* The whole student experience can be summed up by a girl who had been observed in a lesson by a visitor. When the visitor was leaving this girl was obviously not convinced that the messages had got through so she followed the visitor out and took her to one side. She said that if she hadn't decided to try it herself she really should because it was a great way to learn and all schools should do it. For a Year 7 student in her second term this took a lot of courage and belief especially as she hadn't expressed these ideas before. Needless to say we started to use her when visitors came; she would join several others and have lunch and take part in an open forum discussing the new curriculum experience.

This became a regular event but each time we would vary the students, there was no prepping and students had the confidence and belief to express themselves honestly – much to the amazement of the visiting professionals. Eventually we asked ourselves why not use the students to help run the conferences. They were outstanding, giving honest and considered answers to the educational hierarchy without being fazed by the event. They speak in the language we use as professionals, happily explaining and clarifying points much to the surprise of many observers. Over the years they have been able to handle a range of situations from breakfast meetings with industrialists, national launches of educational software, national conferences and local staff development initiatives.

As these visits and conferences became more commonplace so the demand on teachers' time became more pressured – so for one conference a teacher asked the students to prepare a lesson for the next day's conference. Using small groups to brainstorm, an action plan was developed with students taking on the roles and tasks. All of these were completed by the next morning with copies of outlines issued, a video recording made with stops and a summary of each section. The students ran the lesson leaving the teacher to bask in the knowledge that they could be trusted to plan, prepare, learn and teach because they wanted to not because they had to.

Student expectations

Throughout the pilot year we were constantly amazed by the students' ability to rise to the occasion, they were often given work traditionally pitched at Year 9 or Year 10 but because we had taught them how to think, reason and manage information they could assimilate it and succeed. They met me with horror and outrage in Year 8 when they recounted the story that some teachers just gave them books with passages in and activities to complete. And that other teachers told them what to do all the time and never listened to their ideas or comments. We had developed a group of students of whom high expectations were the norm but who also set even higher expectations from their teachers and the interactive education they expected to receive.

From the start of the pilot our expectation for students and from students were raised in line with our ethos; that is to empower them to learn and take responsibility for their learning. What we were in effect doing was to teach and model the teaching strategies which we had developed through time and experience. So when we plan a lesson and go through the resources we reject and identify various sources and pitch work based upon these sources for different abilities and also different outcomes. Nowadays we are likely to set a homework to research a new topic and then, using the school based resources and the student identified resources, we would model the process of valuing and selecting appropriate resources for different outcomes. This then sets a clear model for students to refer back to when handling a resource based task. Not only does this extend the available resources but we have found that it brings excellent first-hand information through direct links from the student's family or friends.

As a student this new curriculum was valued with the most frequent comment being that things made sense and they could see where they were going. Many students felt their 'homework' was valued and had more enthusiasm for it. Homework was changed to work@home.fun during the pilot and is seen as an extension of the lesson with a change in emphasis to the student extending their own learning. Within a short time we had many parents expressing concern over the amount of homework. This came about because teachers set open-ended tasks which students got involved in and they found it hard to stop once they were motivated. One parent went as far as complaining that we were affecting family life as they couldn't go out at weekend until homework was done. Other parents were delighted at being given the opportunity to become part of the learning experience and having a contribution to make.

Student interaction

One very important development was regarding student interaction. Most of the approaches included group-work and we had tried to develop emotional intelligence – students were listening and empathizing with each other. Normally, managing Year 7 would involve a regular stream of students with personal issues such as name calling and in some cases leading up to attendance problems. Tutors and principal tutors would all spend a lot of time repeatedly trying to resolve these problems. Our pilot students were amazing: they didn't report 'issues' because to them they were something to deal with and, having the skills, they just got on with it. The learning experience was very positive so students did not have as much time to make mischief or get involved in issues off task. The respect they had for each other meant that friends and other students would freely voice their opinions, pointing out when someone was acting out of order and standing up for the less-confident student. Fewer issues arose as the students got on better with each other, they were more used to working in a variety of groups not just their narrow friendship set. They listened to each other more and dealt with any issues which arose without recourse to adults or teachers. Occasionally they would deign to let us know that there had been a problem but that it was resolved.

Naturally there were those students who were going to pose problems wherever they were. One student was diagnosed as ADHD and he became the subject of a tutor group action plan where the problems he raised were aired and solutions proposed. The tutor group were then charged with the management of this student which they did admirably without complaint because they understood and empathized with his condition.

> *'Everyone is valued for what they can offer not what they do.'*

> Year 7 student survey

This quote is particularly poignant as it highlights the overall value placed on the contribution of the individual. We have a bright young man who described himself as different to other students. He had worked separately from his peers in his primary school and he recognized a good day's work as pages of writing or calculations. He struggled for the first few weeks as he wasn't used to sharing ideas or working with others to complete a task. He grudgingly praised one teacher by saying that he enjoyed her lessons but didn't think they did any real work. What he meant was that there was no written evidence of the tasks which had taken place and that the skill development was invisible. Under normal systems this boy would have developed some social skills but would have been rather isolated and when he reached university he would probably have had difficulty with basic life skills and common sense solutions to problems. While it took him some time to adjust from a very small primary school to a large comprehensive, he learned to respect all other students in a different way and valued the different outlooks and solutions they were able to offer him.

When the educational psychologist was observing a statemented student with literacy and numeracy problems he could not identify him when he was working in a mixed ability group alongside a boy in the top 5 per cent ability level. Their task was to take four wooden 'buggies' and design a buggy which would be able to overcome difficult terrain and still be able to take a range of experiments no matter what the orientation was. The hands-on approach allowed the statemented student to take the lead and the other students supported and followed his thinking. Only when the task was developed into recording the thinking path did it become apparent who had the literacy and numeracy problems. The students went beyond the labels adults attach to them and used at face value the skills that each person brought to the task.

The development of higher order thinking skills are now evident as the students have been entered into the Citizenship Foundation, Magistrates Court Mock Trial competition. Now in Year 10 the pilot students are thriving within a strong team leading the debating society. It has been a real boon for able and motivated boys to get their teeth into something which is challenging and rewarding. Significantly there are no male students who showed interest from the control group.

The learning experience

By the January of the first year it was clearly evident that we had stumbled upon something special but concerns were being raised about how much higher we could increase our expectation if we used some kind of selection for setting. Three groups were formed, two of 30 and a smaller one of 23. Granham became the upper set, Kingsbury the middle set and Salisbury the smaller targeted group. While the groups were mixed ability there was a good blending of students from all ability ranges. Once the students were in sets they travelled at a pace and in a style more suited to their learning profiles. The faster pace and higher academic expectations for Granham have meant that by the start of Year 9 they were able to start a triple science GCSE course and a maths GCSE course. Kingsbury were also accelerated to a dual science GCSE course. In effect in this area of learning KS3 has been reduced to two years for 74 per cent of the pilot group. The remaining group Salisbury will follow the standard curriculum taking two years to complete the GCSE dual award in science. In other areas it was decided not to start GCSEs early as it was felt that students need higher levels of maturity to do themselves justice in their exams.

As the pilot has progressed we have brought on board students who have entered school mid-year to monitor how they adapt and cope with the change in teaching style and expectation. Of these students there has been a unanimous feeling that they have adapted well without issues arising, and the established students simply paved the way for them by explaining how to do things and how to set about learning. Surprisingly the students are totally unaware of this role but it is an observation which external professionals always comment on: *'They teach each other'* *'they listen and co-operate to plan a task before they start'.*

Interviews with students have confirmed this.

> **Girl** *'We're being taught differently so we learn more easily.'*

> **Boy** *'Good lessons, teamwork, stuff you don't learn normally.'*

Now does that mean the learning isn't normal or that the work goes beyond that normally covered? Either would apply to the St John's experience. The general view from students was that they have learned to:

- enjoy learning
- take responsibility
- think purposefully
- thrive on challenge
- communicate effectively
- work with others effectively
- reflect on issues and make considered judgements
- adapt to changing circumstances.

The enjoyment of the experience was evident both in the behaviour of students in class and around school and as members of the school community. When a survey was conducted on behavioural sanctions such as referrals, lunchtime detentions, after-school detentions and exclusions the differences between the pilot group and the control group were highly significant. Ninety-six per cent of detentions and being sent from lesson were from the control group.

Students were coming into school when ill rather than miss some of their lessons; even reporting sick to the medical room was down to a mere fraction of the other students. Absentees would arrange to get work to friends rather than let them down; email helped with this!

We put this down to their ability to communicate well, emotional literacy and their engagement in their own learning. The students stood out within the school's systems; for instance, when we came to appoint prefects for lower school we had to keep a balance between the students appointed from the control and pilot groups. On interview and letter of application the pilot students were far more capable of presenting themselves and their ideas in a more appropriate way. Once appointed they read more into their responsibilities and often came up with suggestions for improvements in their new roles.

The relationships between both students and students/teachers is significantly different, there is more open dialogue and respect for each others' views. This has given us the opportunity to get the best out of people and situations. Some teachers who came into the pilot in the second and third years felt the students were opinionated and at times arrogant, but others felt that they were using the voice we had given them to question, negotiate and offer suggestions for alternatives. They perceived themselves as equal partners in a learning dialogue.

Comparing research

During research on cognitive testing we videoed some activities so that we could track thought processes. It was more than interesting to see the strategies which students employed to crack codes and come to a solution. There was no need to force them to record their stages they simply used their brains and the materials around them. Some used pencil and paper to record and model the variations, others used tangible objects from their pencil cases, some fingers and some just their intelligence – but which one?

This was then compared to the multiple intelligence work we had done and we discovered they fitted the strategies to their previously identified profile. What we had been doing in the tutorial programme was enabling them to accept that what was right for their learning style was OK. They did not fear ridicule for using fingers (and toes in one case!).

Further into our research (July of Year 1) we also videoed group activities with the pilot group and a control group. Although initially there was the same settling in process as the members of the group gelled and began to contribute, it was clearly evident that the pilot group were more focused and formalized in tackling the problem. They started off with brainstorming then kept stopping to review where they were and check back with the task. Priorities were established and tasks were given a value, the group separated to explore the tasks and then came back together. There was greater evidence of listening skills and support or endorsement from others as points were made. If someone took the task off track there was always another student who would subtly pull it back. Time was not wasted and the learning experience was extended by each person being actively involved in sifting through and rationalizing all contributions.

The control group began in a similar way but took longer to get to a point where they had condensed the problem into tasks. Much of this was because students were undisciplined in their thinking and would throw thoughts out at random. They had not learned to hold the thought and wait until it was relevant, so some channels of enquiry were lost as deflection occurred. It was a much more argumentative group as students tried to take ownership of the 'plum' tasks.

Once on task whether in good grace or bad the students then proceeded to explore the problem. Again the lack of intellectual discipline was evident as some students stayed together and continually interrupted each other as random thoughts came to mind. Fascinatingly one student walked away from the group and went to stand beside the window; this was a boy who was frequently off task and had a very short attention span. The group ignored him and didn't even notice his absence although it went on for several minutes. Suddenly this boy had a surge of energy and bounded back into the fray. The group stopped to accommodate him and he proceeded to pour out his thoughts and ideas in a fairly logical manner. No one interrupted or stopped him and when he had finished they began to unravel it and fit his thoughts into their already half-formed solution. The boy then continued with his normal pattern of behaviour and constantly reiterated the thoughts he had previously expounded. He was not ready to move to the next stage but without his contribution neither would the group have made the progress they did.

What was fascinating is the fact that in a normal classroom situation a student would not have been able to walk to a window and clear his head and mind of the constant noise and distractions. He would have been called back to task and forced to sit in a prescribed place where the conditions evidently failed to match his learning style. Had the teacher known and understood his needs then he would possibly have been more engaged in his learning and not posed the severe disruptive influence he later became.

On comparing the group presentations Year 7s were asked to do, the pilot group showed a confidence and had evidently been familiar with this type of task. They settled to work quickly. Their presentations varied from role play to reading from a script, although there was much ad-libbing the flow continued and they weren't fazed. Everyone was involved and they were very organized. They had a rapport with the audience and didn't concentrate on their crib sheets.

The control group showed mixed levels of enthusiasm, there were several scripted presentations where everyone had lines. The low ability boys were soon distracted and needed encouragement to continue. Some students were left out by groups who had no patience with their attitude and some gave more stilted performances concentrating closely on their scripts. One student shone out from the rest acting as compère, nurturing and encouraging the others.

The pilot group classrooms from the start were easily identified by the levels of noise and often confusion to an outsider's eye. The teacher may be on the floor debating with a group of students; while other students are moving classroom furniture to create their own learning environment, while yet others might step outside the room for the tranquillity of a corridor to be able to sift through and process the task in hand. The pilot group were given the opportunity to explore these variables and subsequently learned to take ownership of the styles which suited them. Students would also quickly learn to adapt to the challenges of mercurial teachers: for several teachers the students would come into class and say 'how do you want us today Miss?' even before they sat down. This was based upon the knowledge that the room, furniture and atmosphere were never constant.

One teacher got the students to bring sheets in and with the candles they had made in another lesson they created a cave and blacked out the windows. They then read extracts from *Beowolf* which became far more vivid and real through this experience (see page 109). This same group desperately wanted to continue learning through their lunch hour and breaks. Their teacher was given the opportunity to check her pigeonhole and answerphone on the strict condition that she hurry back and doesn't stop to talk. Again this reflects the changing relationships with teachers where the joy of learning and the joy of teaching students who want to learn merged into an exciting and rewarding experience for all. This at times takes learning well beyond the prescribed timetable.

The student voice

The student voice has always been important within this initiative not only within a new form of teacher–student relationship but also in a collegiate way where the students felt able to have a say in decision making. Evaluation, which was once done to death, became another version of reflection and students valued the opportunity to mull over and categorize their discoveries. Part of this student voice was recorded by Barrie Wyse, the RSA evaluator:

'Competence skills are what make you different from others.'

'You need skills to get your way around in life, you need to be good at talking and sharing ideas with others when you are set a task and to be able to tackle it and find the easiest source of information.'

'To be part of a group that tries hard and gets along, to be able to watch someone do it and being able to then do it yourself.'

'It gives you a chance to get better results because we are doing Year 8 and Year 9 work in Year 7. A Year 9 boy I know has only just started doing what we did in science this year.'

'Mixing up the subjects is good to help you learn, it seems to make more sense.'

On skills they recognized:

Teamwork, discipline, managing, research, independence, learning how to learn, teaching yourself, thinking of others.

On another survey, students were asked to list the four most important things they had learned since September of that year. This was then carried out with a balanced selection of Years 7, 8 and 9 students. The results when analysed reflected how the skills we had focused upon warranted a value to the student. The pilot group in their responses gave two-thirds of their answers as learning skills to a third of common curriculum experiences. The control group in Year 7 and Year 8 students only had a 1:6 ratio of these skills to curriculum experiences, while the Year 9 students had a 1:15 ratio of the skills to experiences. Year 9s mentioned things such as volleyball, dance, sex education, 8s more rugby skills, making a buzzer, paragraphs, the rainforest, trigonometry.

In December 2002 we had an HMI visit which recognized the strengths of our teaching approach and referred to the sense of excitement and creativity that accompanied it. Particular mention was made of the empowerment of the students within the learning process and the engagement of the parents to support their children's learning.

Pastoral and counselling support

One very positive aspect of the student experience was the change in pastoral and counselling support required. For many years the start of term in September heralded an ongoing series of issues regarding students, settling into their tutor groups and falling out with peers; there were usually several students who had high absence rates and verged on school phobia in the early weeks of transition. As a pastoral team we were very active in instantly assessing the situation and putting in numerous support strategies. As a result Year 7 were allocated additional time with the school's counsellor to meet these needs. In the first year of the pilot these slots were taken up by the control group predominantly with only two students from the pilot using the service in the first term. For the rest of the year the pilot group supported itself raising few issues of this nature and when raised they were quickly discussed by the students and resolutions were found – often without teachers being aware of the problem until later.

In the second and third years of the pilot, when all students were being taught by this approach there was some embarrassment when we couldn't find enough problems to fill the counsellor's Year 7 allocation. In reality this did change over the years but the nature of the problems also changed. We were dealing with far fewer 'quick fix' problems as these were more often being addressed by the students involved. What began to happen was that having tried the initial strategies students came with a greater understanding of what help was needed and they were asking for help to develop and try more sophisticated self-management techniques. We also found a greater willingness to try to help others in similar situations. There was a more open dialogue about past problems and their resolution.

By Years 8 and 9 the students were much more socially aware and ready to step in if they saw a problem. As the Integrated Curriculum unravelled towards Key Stage 4, and the emphasis was upon students employing their skills within the more traditional curriculum structure there was an increase in pastoral problems with some students: these were mainly strong-minded Year 9 girls who brought out-of-school issues into school. Their emotional involvement overrode much of the self-management we had previously seen. This highlighted how successful we had been with the pilot students up to this point and the students who were becoming disaffected were far fewer than we would normally have expected.

The student experience

As we were getting involved in the *Opening Minds* Curriculum, the Council for the Curriculum Examination & Assessment (CCEA) in Northern Ireland was canvassing the opinions of 2,700 KS3 students and teachers on the curriculum. The findings clearly showed that the students asked for coherence; cross-curricular themes were recognized and enjoyed; they disliked repetition; and recognized that assessment was a short-term motivation that had a brief impact but lost the momentum of learning.

Beyond this a *Guardian* poll invited students to write in about their educational experiences and aspirations: 1,500 students responded, calling for 'a school where we learn through experience, experimentation and exploration without a one-size-fits-all curriculum'. A few years ago similar findings were evident when the Industrial Society surveyed 16,000 12–24 year olds. More than two-thirds thought their schooling had failed to equip them with the competences they needed for adult life. They did not think that the National Curriculum and the way schools teach met their aspirations.

The RSA focused on the higher level range of skills for the world of work and beyond, the pace of change and the need for learners to be able to transfer skills in a range of different employment directions. They also looked at redefining work and work patterns to lead the curriculum thinking into relevance for the future citizen.

The research from the CCEA also tells us that pupils are not motivated by the Key Stage 3 curriculum, they cannot identify common skills or links between subjects and they find many subjects insufficiently challenging and of little relevance to their future lives. All in all this leads to the commonly held belief that there is slow progress in the first two years of KS3. Research such as this, alongside the RSA's *Opening Minds* pilot, led to the development in St John's of the Competence Framework and various curriculum initiatives involving 12 partner schools. (In the initial phase, 12 schools were involved; this number fluctuated, reducing to six at one point, before a rapid expansion in the later years of the project.)

Students in this century will not only have to master the current industrial level ICT skills and software but also be able to continue their learning as change takes effect. Ally this to the advances in the science of learning and we are in a much stronger position to create the curriculum for learning. Further, combine with the findings from the Northern Ireland research and a very powerful argument emerges for far greater engagement of students. The simple conclusion is that learning should be relevant and connected: students will learn better when they

- are active and involved;
- can make choices and decisions;
- can learn in different ways;
- can apply their own learning to real life situations.

Where St John's is intrinsically different is that our rationale and objectives are more pupil centred, both in their involvement in the whole process and their ownership of their learning. The analogy often used is like reading a good book: the student is the reader visiting different chapters with themes and experiences that intertwine and enrich the actual experience of learning. The teachers are the writers of the story; each chapter being a progression of the themes and an exploration of more areas for investigation. Occasionally there will be a focal point where the reader needs to turn to one side and further develop his or her skills in order to make more sense of the story. The students have the opportunity to skip pages and veer off in interesting directions if that makes more sense to them.

The fundamental ideas at the core of the St John's Integrated Curriculum:

- Learners must and should be able to take responsibility for their own learning.
- Subject boundaries do not exist.
- The exploration of knowledge, ideas and issues may go in any direction.
- Peer discussion, group-work, reflection and critical thinking should permeate the daily experience.
- Learners are expected to think 'out of the box'.
- Expectations of learners should always be set high by the learners themselves and by their mentor/tutor/teacher.

And, above all,

- Learning is fun and challenging.

Obviously the achievements the students have made have led the decision making and need to be recognized. At the end of the first year we tested all students using Year 7 progress tests and some in-house tests for science and problem solving. Despite following a completely different curriculum, the pilot students scored between 10 and 15 per cent higher in the English, maths, science and a problem-solving test. Within the first two years the pilot group had covered so much of the maths and science curriculum that, of the initial 84 students, up to 60 were in accelerated classes starting GCSEs in maths and science in Year 9. Of the science students, half of them were taking three science subjects in two years, the rest taking double science over the two years. They will sit their GCSEs at the end of Year 10 creating space and choices in the Year 11 curriculum.

The competency framework: teamwork in action

One statemented student who had great difficulty with literacy and numeracy was gaining 56 per cent in an end-of-year, problem-solving test and using geometry in his answers. He had to design a way of measuring the flow of lava from a volcano. Marks were awarded for range of ideas, clarity of communication and viability of ideas. He drew a cross-section of the volcano, he marked distance stages along the trajectory from his viewpoint. He set up a timed photo shoot to measure the distance covered and the speed of flow. To account for the unpredictability of nature he had set up his viewing point from a barricaded site and had in place a back-up plan with a rescue helicopter which would leave the camera transmitting to a satellite. This was all done with minimal text but excellent diagrams and labels.

Throughout there has been a sense of excitement and purpose in the classroom and alongside this there has been a greater level of involvement in the lessons. Students are not taught, they learn – usually for themselves and often along routes they have helped plan. This has meant fewer students who are bored and disruptive, meaning that teachers can really concentrate on the learning and students needs not on dealing with disruptive behaviour. Beyond the classroom the peer relationships have improved as well as the relationships with most teachers. Many teachers value the new relationship as a partnership where each side values and respects the other's contribution.

Don't think that this is all utopia – we still have, and always will have, students who are misguided and bring issues and problems into school. We have many students who have major problems in their home lives which we have to help them manage, but we have found this new curriculum helps all students to support and respect each other. We have been delighted by the growing levels of maturity and responsibility which are clearly seen. An unexpected bonus was the achievement and involvement of the boys, they learned that learning can be fun, it is relevant and you can own parts of it. They lost the 'boffin' syndrome and started to strive for success and then compete – the exact opposite of the national picture where boys' underachievement is such a concern. They are even taking more pride in their work – but unfortunately some of their handwriting is still as bad as it ever was!

It has been difficult to remember the previous St John's experience as the Integrated Curriculum progressed to the Alternative Curriculum and finally was so embedded within our teaching and learning to become the Year 7 Curriculum. It is difficult to state categorically which changes are due entirely to these approaches when cohorts differ so much. For instance, in one of the years we had the highest level of students in one intake with classified emotional and behavioural problems: their impact upon disciplinary measures was significant – but how do you judge whether it might have been worse had we not taught them this way? Certainly the professionals who work with them – educational psychologists, child psychologists and behaviour support teams – report back that they can see a difference in responses; there is less of the self-focusing and more ability to look beyond themselves. This is backed up with parental feedback but they do question whether this was normal maturation rather than educational impact. The parents felt that the pilot students were made to feel special and thus raised self-esteem which had obvious knock-on effects with all-round development.

Summary

It is four years since we launched our first pilot group with our new curriculum. It has evolved since that time but we have retained the fundamental principles which began with the RSA *Opening Minds* Curriculum initiative. We are now firmly committed to a skills led curriculum which empowers students as learners and gives them the skills and experiences to take control of their own learning as a lifelong skill so that whatever needs to be learned at whatever stage in their lives they will be able to learn effectively. We have been travelling in uncharted waters as we developed our approaches and have been very closely monitored at all stages. What has now evolved is a curriculum which we feel best suits the needs of our students as they continue their school experience and move on through their chosen path to higher education or work-based learning. The one constant will be that learning never stops and nor should it.

It has long been recognized that most students can achieve greater success if their education engages them and taps into their individual learning style. With thought and planning it can engage the kinesthetic learner, challenge the gifted and talented, and readily provide alternative routes for those who find it difficult to commit ideas in writing. As students are becoming more aware of their own style of learning they need to have the opportunity to use these strengths to achieve success. From a position of strength they will then be more confident to experiment, take risks and further develop their skills for learning.

Chapter 6

The parents' tale

Kathy Pollard

When we embarked upon the development of our new curriculum we were very aware of the need to engage the parents. A good home–school partnership is one of our foundation stones. Without parents supporting both ourselves and the students we would not be able to break free from the long-established constraints which were entrenched in education. We initiated the involvement of the parents at the June 2001 parents' evening prior to students entering Year 7 in the September. Casual mention was made of St John's educational aspirations and our role at the leading edge of curriculum innovation. At this point the tutor groups had already been established with our standard intake of nine tutor groups. They were in mixed ability groupings although there were two groups with targeted support for the learning needs of some students. To select our three tutor groups for the pilot we ensured that they were representative of the whole intake and mirrored the control group as accurately as our comprehensive data could predict. The parents of selected students within the pilot were invited in for another meeting late in the summer term prior to entry.

The headmaster, Dr Hazlewood, gave a very clear vision of where he saw the education of their children as it now stood and his vision for how he wanted it to develop. This was very well received and provoked lots of response from parents who posed searching and rigorous questions. In its embryonic state with as-yet unformed structures much of what was asked had to be explained with intentions rather than clear systems and procedures. The key features of their concerns revolved around:

- Year 9 preparation for SATs.

- The impact upon GCSE preparation and achievement.

- Will they cover the National Curriculum?

- How will it affect coursework?

- Why change the National Curriculum?

- What forms of assessment will be used?

- Will streaming occur?

These are in the order in which they were asked at the meeting, reflecting a group of parents whose children had just completed booster sessions, extra homework, and the stress and tension culminating in the KS2 SATs. Small wonder that they were responding with the voice which we were trying to eradicate. This is a reflection on a learning experience which drives learning and assessment and takes little notice of the students' needs, strengths and learning styles: the student being processed through the curriculum experience.

As the evening progressed and parents heard the responses to the questions they became more specific to the changes outlined:

- How will you be able to tell if this enthusiastic approach works?

- Will it continue to Year 9 if external funding ceases?

- How soon will the changes take place?

- Will lack of specialization not harm the children?

- What about the teachers – are they willing?

- What about those students who lack motivation and the sense of responsibility to respond fully?

- What about the student who learns better with more structure?

Then came the two critical questions.

- Why are there so few pilot schools if it's such a good idea?

- Is it not a risk?

The evening was a great success in that for once the only topic discussed was the educational experience of students. In the end parents did not want a choice as to whether or not their child would follow the new approaches. The rigorous questioning they posed at times exposed the unformed nature of our plans but revealed our clarity of purpose. Despite being anxious about our lack of a clear structure and the systems which inevitably follow, they were prepared to trust our enthusiasm and willingness to develop and innovate with the student at the centre of our intentions. Parents who were unhappy or unwilling to allow their child to take part were told that they could opt out. There were no such requests! However, within two days there were numerous requests for children to be moved into the pilot groups and the imaginative reasons parents provided showed just how keen they were to justify the inclusion of their child.

Parental liaison has always had a high profile in Year 7. We found that the control group contacts were as they always had been – phoning in about friendship problems, issues on the buses, locker keys going missing, lost property or the poor choice of menu. Worryingly we were not hearing from the parents of our pilot students – we waited with bated breath. Discreetly we started to look at the reasons why this might be happening, The first idea was too radical to pursue, that is that the parents had nothing which they felt required additional input. This ran into the thoughts that perhaps they were holding back and giving us some breathing space to develop our new skills based curriculum. When questioned the students readily admitted that they had the same issues but instead of going home to parents with their problems they were either dealing with them directly or using the teachers to help resolve them. It was already obvious that the approach was creating a better student–teacher relationship – but would this be recognized and valued by the parents?

Within the first term we normally send home a transition review and there is often contact between tutors and parents to resolve any issues. Most of the tutors continued to respond to parental contacts in the usual way but the three tutors of the pilot group had far fewer contacts with parents and felt that students were making a very positive transition. At this point we had already seen the results of empowerment through skill development but it was too early to be making claims. There were already clear indications that students were much more focused and behavioural issues had virtually disappeared within the pilot group lessons.

We hesitantly started to murmur that the boys seemed to be much more engaged and were achieving far higher than was the previous norm. Gone was the 'it's not cool to succeed or be recognized for doing well'. Success was celebrated, healthy competition was re-emerging and higher aspirations were being set from both students and teachers. Much of this was brought to our attention from comments by parents.

This was further endorsed on parents' evenings when conversations revealed how much a teacher had influenced and inspired their children. For the first time parents of Year 7 students were not focusing upon their child's happiness as the first priority. In a more bizarre way this also made dialogue with parents more complex. Teachers were challenged if they made comments about how a child was struggling with a task, it was pointed out by parents that '... *was a kinesthetic learner with a strong bias towards interpersonal skills and had this been taken into account?*' Or '*Why do you expect the task to be completed in that way when ... has always said that he finds it easier to produce it as a storyboard?*'

Whenever there was contact with parents they were keen to make known their pleasure in the way their child was responding to the new curriculum. Students who had recognized behavioural problems in primary school apparently 'disappeared without trace' in secondary school, because the learning environment was so positive. With peer engagement a key priority, most who had 'problems' just got on with the tasks in hand because it was fun and exciting to learn this way.

Parents were extremely helpful in notifying us of emerging issues. Initially, to integrate the storyline and remove subject boundaries, we issued files with dividers for different teachers but Year 7 students found the management of this was too difficult and pages were being misfiled, papers were getting lost and concerns were raised. We rapidly responded and issued books for each teacher's area of the curriculum (see page 45). We later had some concerns voiced about modern foreign languages which we recognized needed addressing and again valued the contributions parents made, helping us to see the knock-on effects of our innovation.

Parents' questionnaire

After five months we had our annual parents' evening for all Year 7 students. The control group parents made appointments with subject teachers and tutors as usual. The parents of the pilot students met the teachers who had taught their child up to Christmas. At this time the teaching teams rotated each term. Without fail the parents commented upon how well the teachers knew their child, his or her best learning style and their individual strengths and weaknesses. Some were still anxious about individual subject National Curriculum levels and others tried to unravel the links to get subject specific information. All parents were positive and pleased with the start of the pilot. Following our usual procedure we asked parents to complete a questionnaire on the school and educational provision. This is always analysed and feeds into reviews on policy and provision.

The views quoted on page 92 represent the whole cohort six months into their first year at the school and many of the comments will be familiar to all educational establishments.

The tutors' perceptions of parents' views from the parents' evening were that there was very positive feedback and a genuine interest in the pilot as well as in their child's general progress.

Amalgamated quotes from parents' questionnaire – comments in January of the first year (2002)

Our strengths were recognized as providing:

Supporting role for parents and pupils. A happy secure atmosphere. Good public relations. Care for all its pupils and treating children as individuals. Pastoral care reflects values. Openness.

Teachers are very approachable and more than happy to help with problems. Good quality of teaching staff. Well organized. A clear ambition to improve the school and students. Consistent high standards and expectations. High standards of teaching, A strong sense of identity. Academic. Good discipline and conduct. Focus on child's requirements not academic excellence.

Emphasis on building a child's sense of personal responsibility and self-reliance. Forward thinking. Continually wanting to improve. Experiences linked to knowledge. Encouraging learning in a dynamic way.

Interestingly they suggested these as the main areas for improvement:

Less homework / more homework. Subjects not challenging enough.

More effort should be made for spelling.

Communication with parents. Making parents' evening appointments should be done by the school not the students. The system for contacting teachers about concerns should be clearer. It would be helpful to have parents' evenings once a term with reports prior to parents' evenings. Information to parents could be spread more evenly over the school year. More access to parents to view displays. More notice should be given for forthcoming events.

A single site school, extra resources, support staff and equipment.

Waiting for buses after school – who is responsible for children if buses are late?

School building looks shabby and dated. Toilets are unsatisfactory. Buses between sites.

Lack of lockers. More flexibility on dining arrangements. Why do the children have to queue for so long at lunch?

More suitable school trousers for girls and they should all wear the same. The school dress code could be more strongly adhered to.

Disruptive pupils should be removed from classes.

Mixed feelings about the way pupils behave out of school while still in uniform.

Better range of non-sporting extra-curricular activities. More encouragement to do extra activities. More emphasis on developing one sport.

Again these responses fed into self-evaluation systems, and responses to many issues were conveyed via the monthly newsletter. We took advantage of this evolving relationship with parents and invited them to become partners in reviewing the school's policies; several became engaged in this and were seen redrafting policies in line with the changing face of St John's and the society in which we find ourselves.

Parental concerns

By mid-year it was decided that the mixed ability groups had been very successful but that we had developed the more able learners to the point where we believed that they could learn more effectively in ability groups. We created three sets within the pilot to a great deal of parental concern. The groups were given geographical names to avoid any signs of rank order (see page 50).

Two key issues arose: firstly, parents wanted to know how and why students had been allocated to each **ability group**. Our decisions were not just based upon ability but on engagement with learning, and the ability to run with it. When parents were given a description of a student who once given a learning structure could and would succeed, they readily agreed that described their child. It was when we then asked could your child take a problem, create a research plan, carry it out, refine and disseminate the information appropriately for the end function – they then realized how the learning styles affected the setting arrangements and grudgingly agreed that the proposed teaching approach was the one most suited to their child. This reinforced our decision to set those who were autonomous learners and could run with their own development while those who needed a little more structure were taught how to create effective structures for learning by modelling the skills for them to replicate and practise independently. The fact that the students could and did end up achieving at a similar academic level did not always mollify them.

The second key issue parents raised was regarding the **break-up of friendships** formed in the first term. To resolve this students were taught in their sets but went back to the tutor group for tutorials, PE and House matches. Several parents expressed grave concerns and predicted students would be unsettled and wanted us to teach some lessons in tutor groups putting friendship groups before learning styles and academic progress. This would have compromised our learning styles approach but in reality within two to three weeks the students settled and had no further problems with this arrangement. Several parents came back and reported that not only had their child maintained the previous friendships but increased their support base with new friends. It needs to be said that several of the key staff were also expressing concern and were ready to fight the parents' case if necessitated by problems arising from the setting. They too were among the first to recognize the positive effects of the new arrangements.

As the years progress parents have been confused by our approach to **homework** and, as with many schools, we have found this difficult to resolve as feedback comes from both ends of the spectrum. One change we made was to change the emphasis from homework to work@home.fun, this being seen as a natural extension of the learning taking place in the classroom, the student taking aspects forward or preparing for the next day's lessons. Many parents request more homework in an effort to get their child to make as much progress as possible within a structured programme. At the other extreme we have parents who are much more vociferous, claiming that we set far too much homework and that their own lives and the lives of the children are adversely affected by the strain this puts upon them. In line with our philosophy that the student is in partnership with the teacher to develop their own learning we encourage students to extend themselves and they very often get carried away by the satisfaction they experience. Work is done to a far higher standard than we would have expected and obviously takes longer, but the sense of pride with which that student returns the work is immeasurable.

Another issue we have had to deal with is to do with assessment of work. If a student has spent hours on a piece of work they do not want to see red ink all over it with corrections. Verbal feedback and peer assessment are not visible formats and so parents have felt that work is unmarked and not getting the recognition which the effort merited. As with all educational experiences the tension between producing hard data for quantifiable measures cannot be matched by the soft data which reflects a qualitative experience, yet this is what we are trying to achieve.

The interactions with parents continued to be monitored and reviewed into the second and subsequent years of the project. There was a significant increase in responses which linked to our new provision. We are used to the usual positive affirmation of good practice and the equally regular grumbles about personal issues but in this analysis there was a definite change of focus and terminology. The anonymity of the parents prevents clear identification but we had rarely come across comments of this nature and certainly not in this quantity before.

Parents made much greater reference to:

- Encouragement of learning in a much more dynamic way.

- High standards, expectations and ambition for the school and students.

- Strong focus on the students/their needs, emphasis on personal responsibility and self-reliance.

- Recognition of many of our strengths, that is support, teamwork, values, accessibility, approachability and good public relations.

There are many more but these were the ones which directly related to our aspirations.

Interestingly the main areas they identified for improvement continued to be focused upon systems, uniform, buses, meals and behaviour. There wasn't a single comment relating to curriculum or learning/teaching style after the first term. Students also reported some frustration with parents who kept trying to unravel the learning experience asking what had they done in maths or science. All of these interactions reinforced our belief that this curriculum approach was working for the students and parents were still supporting us.

	Beginning of Year 7		End of Year 7	
	Pilot	**Control**	**Pilot**	**Control**
Willing or Enthusiastic	77	76	91	87
Enthusiastic	34	62	84	32
Enthusiastic to learn	+50%	-30%		
Willing or Enthusiastic	+20%	+11%		

	Pilot	Control
Enthusiastic to learn	+50%	-30%
Willing or Enthusiastic	+20%	+11%

Statistics

At the end of the first year, reports and an anonymous parental questionnaire were sent out. After a year of the Integrated Curriculum the swing towards enthusiastic learners was significant. At the upper end both control and pilot groups increased their overall attitude to learning.

The large increase in the pilot from willing to enthusiastic to learn of +50 per cent probably indicates high motivational factors for learning; conversely, in the standard approach to the National Curriculum enthusiasm for learning in the control group fell significantly.

At the opposite end of the scale, parents reported 15 per cent of the control group were classed as 'passive learners' or those who needed 'to be pushed' to achieve compared to 7.5 per cent in the pilot group.

Homework	% of pilot group	% of control group
Able to work willingly and easily	60	27
Need structure to work independently	31	50

Homework is often the source of conflict in the home when parents start to try to support students in their learning. The impact of willing workers who were more independent meant less tensions at home over home and school work.

When looking at students' ability to learn, parental responses indicate that 79 per cent of the pilot either do so effortlessly or with effort with none giving up. The control group were at 74.5 per cent with 7.5 per cent giving up. Again this reflects a slight improvement in attitude but with a definite engagement of those at the lowest end.

Parental comments for students in the pilot clearly reflect actual techniques such as learning strategies, mind maps, visual and aural styles, hands-on learning, practical involvement, clear focus, pairs and group-work being particularly noted. Parents of the control group had more negative comments recorded, for example, 'lacks understanding', 'needs things explaining', 'dislikes silent working environment', 'can't remember what it meant'.

When it came to taking responsibility both groups reflected similar responses but when doing so without prompting the pilot group scored 64 per cent compared with the control group at 14 per cent. This reinforces the expectation factor – the students are capable of taking more responsibility if given the opportunity. Where the pilot students excel is in taking responsibility for themselves, putting into practice the skills they have developed.

Parents who had had a child already go through the school were asked to compare their experiences at St John's: 14 thought the pilot experience was more positive, 7 similar, in the control group 13 responses indicated a similar picture. Reassuringly this reflects the school's efforts to strive for the highest standards, continuously monitoring and trying to improve the students' experience in school. Finally parents were asked to make any comments on the educational experience for their child. This question allowed free rein to parents to express concerns and a range of issues were identified. It is pleasing to note that there were twice the number of positive responses from parents of pilot students and only two-thirds the number of negative responses compared to the control group.

Parental contacts have continued to be very positive but the differences between the control group and the pilot group have diminished somewhat as we as teachers have automatically and at times deliberately extended the approach to all our classes minimizing the level of contrast.

Sadly some parents of the control group felt that their children were marginalized by the experience and that they had had a second-class educational experience. As stated earlier, they felt that the self-esteem of the pilot students was raised by their being made to feel special which had further influenced all-round development. They commented that the control group were disadvantaged. Unfortunately, our efforts to communicate the fact that we were, from the start of Year 8, teaching the control group about learning styles and empowering them to take more control of their learning was not communicated well enough. Perhaps by this time a level of learned dependency was established which inhibited the development of autonomous learning in this group. It was particularly felt by parents that the more gifted and talented students in the control group had been disadvantaged. Despite opportunities being open to all fewer of them took advantage. This included volunteering to take extra responsibilities such as peer mentoring, acting as prefects, bus monitors and running the fair trade shop. We have had to take great care to appoint a representative range of students without bias towards those already empowered who outshone others at interview.

It should be noted that this feeling of 'missing out' by the control group parents has continued throughout the four years. At various stages there has been criticism of neglecting the control group. As the results of the pilot came through we were very aware that we were morally bound to employ some of the successful strategies for the control group. We redesigned the tutorial programme to empower the control group with the same learning skills both in Year 8 and Year 9. Despite this, parents kept asking for their children to be moved to the pilot group who they perceived as having a more exciting learning style. This was in part the result of the students' own enjoyment of their lessons which was reflected in conversations and actions over the year. The combination of willing learners and committed teachers was visibly recognized by parents and visitors to the school.

Another perspective we have taken into account in our review of parental interaction has been the responses from parental visitors looking around the school during the working day. Without fail they comment upon the buzz and the focus on learning. They also dare to mention that the classes seem to be noisier with which we fully agree; classes that are engaged are often so involved that they don't hear the bell and at times even the teacher's voice. One parent was very surprised when a child without even looking up said 'just a minute I need to finish this', little realizing they were talking to the headteacher and a visitor.

Parents have taken great pride in the unexpected bonuses linked to the curriculum innovation, which have involved students speaking at conferences, leading discussion groups, being involved in hands-on practical research, and the more exciting ones with breakfast meetings with industrialists and presentations in London at a variety of venues. Visitors to the classrooms and school are the norm rather than an interruption to normal activities.

One area on which we had some response was the pupil behaviour and support systems. Parents of the pilot students simply did not need these extra supports as the students were not presenting problems as they would normally have done. As the previous section explained, behaviour and attendance improved to such an extent that apart from one boy with very extreme needs there were no external or internal exclusions, detentions were a rarity and students did not get sent out of class for poor behaviour or disruption. Naturally parents were pleased but they were not aware what a difference this was from the norm established in school over the years. The impact of this upon parents has been that there has been far less need for additional meetings and interventions even as the students have passed through the trauma of adolescence and the challenges they usually present.

Throughout the evolution of this project we have continued to rely upon parental feedback as correlation of our perspective and have valued the input they have made. One factor we should have responded to was for more frequent updates on the progress of the pilot both within St John's and within the national and international arenas. We were hesitant to oversell our successes and to keep reinforcing the differences between our two groups of students was not what we felt to be in their best interests. We were very aware that some parents were feeling aggrieved at having missed out on the opportunity for their child.

Reports

Reports have been the greatest trial of the whole system. We very much feel that we should be reporting to parents upon the competences and skill development minimizing the focus upon National Curriculum levels. Unfortunately human nature comes into play and most parents (including senior staff whose own children were in the new curriculum) went straight for the hard data, that is, the improvement in National Curriculum levels and in test scores. The hours teachers had spent reviewing progress within the competence framework was the section which was read last and even then parents tried to unravel it into subject areas. We then questioned whether we had been getting the message across effectively. Students were delighted with the comments and felt they were spot on in describing their progress and they did eventually feel that parents saw this reflection of the child in the report. The reports have evolved in line with our greater confidence on reporting valid and worthwhile data but recognizing that parents do want the subject skills to be clearly recognized. Each year we have refined the format until we have come up with our current style (see pages 98–102). This starts off with an overview of the student and his or her learning. Comments are made within the key section of the skills we are developing, finishing with brief sections from each of the subject teachers. This too may change as our now-established St John's curriculum continues to evolve.

It was noticeable that after the first set of reports were sent home fewer parents made appointments for the extra parents' evening we put on. The reasons given were that the information the report contained so fully described their child that there wasn't a need to discuss it further.

One factor with which we cannot comply is the request to have termly reports followed by termly parents' evenings. We already have three parents' evenings: one prior to entry in the June, one in September to meet the tutors and hear more about the curriculum approaches and a formal one in February. We report home informally in the November and formally in June. This request probably reflects the difference in relationships between parents and teachers in primary schools and the secondary school. Primary schools are in the immediate locality where daily access is available to address needs, and contact is easy as pupils usually require to be escorted to home and school each day. The less intense relationship when a student travels out of the immediate locality to the 'big school' creates an invisible barrier to accessing teachers and parents often feel out of the loop. At St John's we try very hard to maintain the friendly open-door approach where parents feel that they can contact us at any time.

It is, perhaps, an obvious point but we strongly believe that engagement with parents, providing very clear lines of communication, allows parents to have an interactive role in evaluating what the school is trying to achieve. This feedback allows parental views to have an impact on the curriculum direction. With supportive parents, engaged students and an enthusiastic teaching force anything is achievable.

Letter to Parents

It gives me pleasure to enclose your child's Year 7 Report. This year's format has been improved as a result of parental feedback last year. We hope that this report gives you a clear and detailed picture of your child's progress at St John's.

To many of you the layout of this report will be unfamiliar but it is appropriate that the values we attach to the skills that underpin our Alternative Curriculum are clearly recognised in the body of the report. The competence assessments which follow the Learning Manager's comments are the result of close collaboration between staff and students using both formal and self-assessment procedures.

Teacher assessed National Curriculum levels have been given in English, Mathematics and Science. These levels are based on achievement in a range of activities covering some of the Key Stage 3 curriculum. After the Key Stage Level indicated you will see the letter 'a', 'b' or 'c'. The letter 'a' means that your child has generally produced work at the upper end of the level, a 'b' means work achieving the middle level and 'c' means work produced at the lower end of the level.

There are comments on your child's achievements in the different curriculum areas and the Year 7 Report concludes with information relating to attendance. Should there be any unauthorised absences please contact me with an explanation in order that your child's record can be updated.

Yours sincerely

Mr M More
Principal Tutor - Year 7

KEY STAGE 3 REPORT

St John's School & Community College
Marlborough

Toby

7 A

Reporting Period 2004 - 2005

LEARNING MANAGER'S COMMENTS

Comments:

Toby has been a delightful and reliable member of the tutor group this year. He has represented Avon house in the inter-house sports matches for rugby and football and has attended a lunchtime computer club. He has been awarded a bronze certificate for the number of merits he has received since September. He has a positive attitude to learning and is generally very well behaved. He puts a pleasing level of effort into all his work. Toby is a caring and sympathetic student and is a valued member of the tutor group with good interpersonal skills He particularly enjoys working with numbers and musical and artistic activities.

Targets:

1. Avoid any kind of distraction.

2. Improve the accuracy of his written work.

3. Maintain his positive attitude in year 8.

Learning Manager: Mrs A Gilder   May 2005

St John's School and Community College

SCHOOL ATTENDANCE

Number of ½ days in reporting period	
Number of ½ day absences	26
Number of ½ day unauthorised absences	0

SENIOR MANAGEMENT TEAM'S COMMENTS

An excellent report. Well done.

SMT Member Dr P K Hazlewood   May 2005

YEAR 7 PRINCIPAL TUTOR'S COMMENTS

Congratulations Toby on this high quality and thoroughly deserved excellent report. Maintain your current diligent and enthusiastic standards and further advances will occur. Well done indeed!

Principal Tutor: Mr M More   May 2005

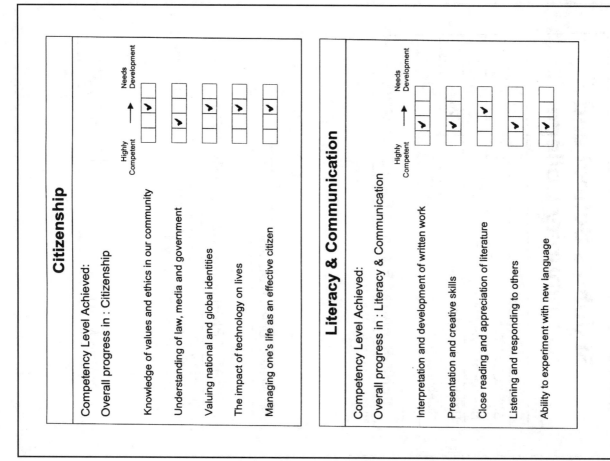

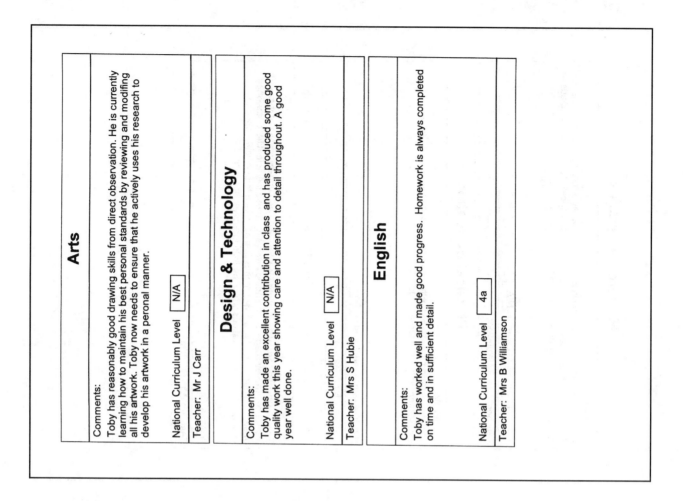

Arts

Comments:
Toby has reasonably good drawing skills from direct observation. He is currently learning how to maintain his best personal standards by reviewing and modifing all his artwork. Toby now needs to ensure that he actively uses his research to develop his artwork in a peronal manner.

National Curriculum Level   N/A

Teacher: Mr J Carr

Design & Technology

Comments:
Toby has made an excellent contribution in class and has produced some good quality work this year showing care and attention to detail throughout. A good year well done.

National Curriculum Level   N/A

Teacher: Mrs S Hubie

English

Comments:
Toby has worked well and made good progress. Homework is always completed on time and in sufficient detail.

National Curriculum Level   4a

Teacher: Mrs B Williamson

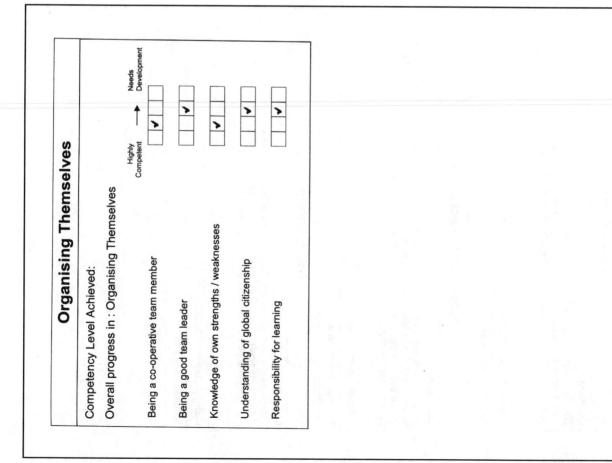

Organising Themselves

Competency Level Achieved:

Overall progress in : Organising Themselves

Highly Competent ———→ Needs Development

Being a co-operative team member

Being a good team leader

Knowledge of own strengths / weaknesses

Understanding of global citizenship

Responsibility for learning

Modern Languages

Comments:
Toby has been working well in class, especially when sitting apart from those who distract him. He is becoming more confident when speaking and he now needs to improve the accuracy of his written work.

National Curriculum Level   N/A

Teacher: Mrs G Hazlewood

Physical Education

Comments:
Toby has shown high levels of effort and participation this year, including involvement in house tournaments.

National Curriculum Level   N/A

Teacher: Mr A Maxwell

Science

Comments:
Toby is working hard at developing his knowledge and understanding of the work introduced in Key Stage 3. He should always try to use the scientific ideas when answering questions. He takes a methodical approach to practical work and makes relevant observations which he then interprets successfully.

National Curriculum Level   5a

Teacher: Mrs C White

Humanities

Comments:
Toby is always enthusiastic and works well in Humanities. He needs to contribute more to class discussions. His level of subject knowledge and understanding is good. Information management is one of his developing strengths.

National Curriculum Level   N/A

Teacher: Mr G Ditchburn

Information Technology

Comments:
Toby is a confident user of ICT and is developing good practical skills, together with a sound knowledge and understanding of the subject. To progress further he should start to independently explore higher level functions of the various software applications.

National Curriculum Level   N/A

Teacher: Mrs C White

Mathematics

Comments:
Toby is a conscientious worker. He has the basic numerical skills needed for success. He now needs to build on this by applying those skills in different areas. He needs to ensure that work is always completed to the best of his ability

National Curriculum Level   4a

Teacher: Mr A Ellis

Chapter 7

The curriculum in practice

From the preceding chapters the development and implementation of the 'new' curriculum through the eyes of those involved has unfolded. For the practitioner, however, the question is invariably 'what does it actually look like in the classroom?'; this is usually followed by 'where do I find this?'. We have been very careful in all of the conferences and visits for the many hundreds interested in our work not to be prescriptive. Whatever you do in your school must be right for you; it depends on the staff profile, the response of the children, the resources available and the degree of risk that you are prepared to take! The examples below outline a variety of lessons created by the authors. They are but a tiny snapshot of the curriculum experience; they are not the 'best', but ones that have been developed in conjunction with the children and that give a flavour of the Integrated Curriculum approach. The teachers' perspective on the frame of the lesson(s) precedes the outline.

A view of the Forests Module

Kathy Pollard

A critical part of the teaching and learning process has been the interaction between the lessons throughout the day, week and module. This was planned in advance by the team of teachers responsible for the module delivery. Initially this was without any reference to the National Curriculum. As previously mentioned, as the pilot progressed we began to realize that we were not only covering the work normally associated with Year 7 students, but were stretching them to understand and work at levels far above their chronological age. It was not unusual for students to be covering the same work as their older siblings in Years 9 or 10.

There was an acknowledgement that at times discrete lessons would be needed to ensure full understanding of a concept, principle or process. Similarly, by the second year we realized that the freedom the pilot group had been given to take risks would have to be managed in some way so that all students had a common core of essential curriculum skills. Each group of students has their own strengths and diversity of learning styles that will affect their response to learning. This in turn guides the learning journey for that class.

As outlined earlier, 'The Book' that travels around with the students is critical to ensuring that teachers are aware of the progress of the learning journey and also any diversions or detours that may have taken place on the way. The teacher needs to be ready to modify the starting point from the stage the students have reached in the previous lessons and not from where the teacher thought they may be!

Forests Module: identifying trees

The example that follows illustrates the interlinking of the curriculum strands organizing information, managing situations, relating to people and citizenship.

The approach to the Forests Module is usually in the form of an agreed extended assignment which integrates each of the curriculum areas. The brief begins:

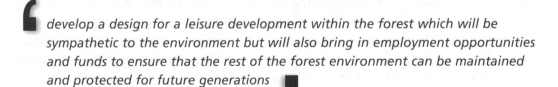

develop a design for a leisure development within the forest which will be sympathetic to the environment but will also bring in employment opportunities and funds to ensure that the rest of the forest environment can be maintained and protected for future generations

Tasks should include the production of a submission of an outline plan for the council to consider. It will need to meet simplified planning regulations for siting, environmental considerations, access, a full business plan of proposed facilities and marketing proposals including multilingual brochures.

The maths specialist would start the lesson off recapping the points the students had reached last week leading them to the focus for the current lesson. This would be looking at area, space, ratio and scale. A proactive approach was used for students to experience real applications including measuring objects as varied as bus passes, desks, a mobile classroom and a tennis court. With real examples students would then develop the skills to deal with problems associated with measurements and representation.

As the class moves on to the next teacher, who happened to be a geography and ICT teacher, the students were introduced to contour maps of the school and the local environment which includes the nearby forest. The use of scale and proportion on the map is studied and representation of local features is explored. The symbols and graphics are considered and left until later on in the module when students will create their own maps developing their own graphics. Visualization of the information from the map involves students developing insight into the varied environments and consideration of the historical influences on those environments.

The day progresses with a science input in which students go out into the forest to carry out some experiments they have designed in the previous week. Part of the focus of the journey will be to identify the landmarks and features which are on the maps the students carry. Similarly the range of habitats and environments will be at close quarters and then extended as the students become aware of the diversity of the creatures and people who occupy this area. Having carried out the experiments and recorded the results in their own formats, the students are given time over lunch to further explore the area. As they do this they are able to collect limited samples of colour and texture on which to build their next lesson.

Forests Module: writing up results

After their return to school, lessons resume in an art room. The focus here is to bring the collected samples and ideas from the forest to identify the diversity of colours and textures in the forest environments. Using the extended terminology, and developing the skills to portray these, will enable students to bring creativity to the fore. As the day concludes the students move on to another teacher, this time for a design and technology input. Depending upon the ideas developed by the particular learning group, the work may then go in one of several ways. Students may work in groups on breaking down the key task and tackling aspects of it; some students may be working on the siting of the development and creating graphical representation based upon the work from the beginning of the day. Others would examine the provision of accommodation and siting, trying to avoid damage to the environment identified in lessons two and three. Some would focus on the individual units looking at suitable materials to use for harmony, colour and texture in building materials for the development. Those who prefer to be more creative might take the interior design of units looking at décor and design, again tapping into the forest features, the drawing skills and terminology.

As the module progresses ICT will be used to scan designs to develop scale and vary motif size, tiling for wallpaper, producing fabric transfers for wall hangings and curtains. Another group would look at provision of sympathetic catering facilities; they would examine the provision for residents and staff as well as day visitors. Menus would focus on forest fare and healthy options. Again development of ideas would include experimenting with basic recipes, trying variations to create a changing but manageable menu which reflects the changing environments and seasons. This work continues through the module increasing in depth and complexity, challenging the students to go well beyond the boundaries imposed by the normal curriculum.

Students' responses to this activity set on their doorstep have enabled them to use family and friends to help them develop and refine ideas. Some do formal presentations of the whole range of tasks, others hold a public debate with students representing interested parties, local people, the planning committee, environmentalists, people with disabilities, tourists, and so on. All identify more fully with the issues integrated into their own learning as they have greater involvement in the direction of the journey. This varies from an amble along a country lane to 'fast tracking' via a four lane motorway. They never reach journey's end as every corner opens up new learning opportunities. A true reflection of the lifelong learning approach we hope to inspire.

Making the News Module – Charity campaigns (after the tsunami)

Richard Smith

The following description details a single lesson, one which formed part of a sequence in the Year 7 module, Making the News. Although the tasks, the challenges and the results are pertinent to this one particular session, the ethos is characteristic of all our Year 7 *Opening Minds* Curriculum lessons.

Should you happen to get the chance to observe my class of Year 7 students 'in action' with the *Opening Minds* Curriculum, there would be much which may catch your attention: their friendliness; their eagerness to work together; their increasingly mature approach to their own learning; their determination to achieve; their sense of ownership of their own work. But above all this I know that the first thing which you would notice is the diversity within the group – in their backgrounds, their academic ability and their approach to work. However, what I love about this group is that they are progressively more and more able to build positively upon this diversity, to 'pool' their individual skills and knowledge in order to learn together.

Prior to this particular lesson the students had begun working upon launching a charity campaign: in answer to their interest in and concern for the tsunami disaster of 26 December 2004, we planned a sequence of lessons together in which the students would be able to create, design and launch a charity campaign, one which would raise public awareness of the devastating and far-reaching effects of the tsunami, while also persuading a target audience to donate money. I had had a totally different sequence of lessons in mind… but they argued that this was an important issue and they wanted to explore it. And to achieve this they decided that they would work in mixed-gender, mixed-ability groups of their own choosing. (A bossy lot, huh?)

On this particular day I arrived at my lesson early since, as usual, four or five of the students rush energetically into the classroom well before the lesson is due to start because they want to 'rearrange the tables' for the group-work; I take this as an opportunity to begin to write the lesson aims out on the board only to find another student – who has also arrived early – enthusiastically offering to finish the task for me (*'aren't we working on our group skills and persuasive skills, Sir?'*). Soon I find that even though the lesson has not yet 'officially' begun, the majority of my class have already arrived, organized themselves back into their groups, unpacked, distributed activity sheets I had prepared, relieved me of any other small tasks I may have had to complete… and begun the lesson themselves. As I listen to them instantly chattering about their campaigns – noting that it is still one minute before the lesson starts – instead of feeling redundant, I simply feel as though I am part of a team, a single cog in a well-oiled machine.

Their first activity involved each group member presenting their 'homework' to the rest of their team: this formed the basis of a discussion which both addressed what problems were encountered and how these were overcome, and also identified what elements of the campaign still needed further work and the prioritizing of these. Should this already sound demanding enough, I shall also point out that these were individual 'homework' tasks which were chosen and assigned by the group in the previous lesson, each one designed to help move the project towards completion. (I shall gloss over, here, the fact that the previous lesson also finished with a number of students asking if they could spend *'longer than half an hour on [their] homework?'*).

So our class is now filled with the chatter of 30 11-year-old students eagerly explaining why they *'researched this'*, *'drew that'*, *'decided to improve this chart'* and *'wrote another two scripts for our radio advert'*. The lesson had begun in its usual noisy manner (we, as a class, had recently spent some time exploring Neil Mercer's (2000) work based upon group discussion, and the students are now always keen to 'discuss' anything at any time without even the slightest hint of a need to do so!), and since 90 per cent of the groups are working perfectly well without me, I am able to return to a smaller group of three students with whom I had begun some guided support work.

And so our lesson continued: each student totally absorbed in his or her own task (after all, why not? – they had each discussed where their individual strengths lay, what they could offer to the team, and how they would like to contribute to the group). Unlike other classes from older year groups, as I support my guided students I feel no concerns that the majority of the class may wander off task, since the relaxed, yet productive mood which pervades the lesson is punctuated only occasionally by one student reproaching another to *'work harder'* or to explain why they are not being 'more constructive'. At one point I see one of my livelier students heading from her own group towards another… is she attempting to defect, I wonder? No, her group have asked her to show prototype charity catchphrases around the room to gauge public reaction.

As I step back for a moment and observe this hive of activity, once again it is the strong sense of diversity which strikes me: two highly able students are heatedly debating whether posters or leaflets would be most persuasive; another girl with strong intrapersonal skills looks up from her writing and gently encourages a fellow group member as he nervously, yet proudly, continues to design a charity logo; a normally shy boy is animatedly explaining to anyone in his group who will listen how he would like his radio script to sound; a 'statemented' student is increasingly getting to grips with the stopwatch I have given him, and he is going from group to group telling them how much time they have left for this section of the lesson; and while one girl tells her group *'we have to use more personal pronouns'*, one of my guided students zips across the classroom to grab a dictionary *('I want to see how to spell* adult*')*.

At times we pause for a moment, the students freezing in position, looking to read the body language of their group members, seeking to identify from facial expressions and physical attitude who is feeling confident, who is feeling demotivated, who needs further encouragement. Later on a number of groups, those who are clearly thriving on the multifarious nature of the task, are given an additional challenge: I create a 'bank account' with a credit balance already in place for them; however, I also give them a price list, detailing the production costs of the various posters, TV adverts and radio announcements which they are creating. Now they have to bring budgeting into the equation, and elect a finance manager to oversee spending. It was at this point that the conversations intensified… greatly. So too did my smile: the noise, the conversations and the actions told me that the students were clearly enjoying themselves.

Our lesson drew to a close with five (self-elected) students pitching their campaigns to the other groups, explaining their ideas and then asking for constructive feedback as a means of refining the campaign further still, before then taking these comments back to their own team. The plenary (and this really should be no surprise when I say this) is delivered by the students: the five envoys confidently outline to the whole class the various pieces of advice and criticism which they have received, explaining to everyone how each group can work together to take their projects towards completion.

As the students supervise each other packing away, quietly telling each other *'you need to finish that picture by next lesson'* / *'I shall get some more information for us all to use'*, I once again realize that my role within this class / team has not been that of a teacher, I am simply another member of their group. And that feels good.

Making sense of the theory – Making the News Module: *Beowolf* (an English lesson)

Lyn Quantick

The strength and depth for the learning of Year 7 students relies on several pieces of the curriculum puzzle being in place.

- The lesson needs to be led by the competences (skills) but delivered through the subjects;

- The teachers need to have the overview of how each subject dovetails and supports the others;

- The lessons need to be part of the whole module journey, the teacher and the students both being clearly aware of what has happened elsewhere in the module;

- Our curriculum, as well as the Key Stage 3 Strategy, encourages and supports the notion that the journey, not the arrival, underpins the whole learning experience;

- As teachers we will move into any subject that will help to tell our stage of the journey.

In order to bring the theory of the competence based curriculum to life, looking at a lesson along the learning journey – in this case an English lesson within Making the News – may clarify what ingredients make up the experience for a Year 7 student.

The students had already spent time looking at methods of communication through the ages which were discussed and put into a historical timeline. They looked at the media, focusing on newspapers, radio and television. Creating their own TV news broadcast and assessing the daily newspapers had allowed them to use their acquired skills to produce work, based on the living world of 21st-century media. This allowed them to develop their own opinions about how news events were portrayed which in turn were supported by their 'new-found' knowledge. This knowledge encompassed approaches to news gathering, journalistic interpretation, creating a story, factual reporting and synthesis of information to distort the actual facts of what makes news. Therefore they were able to bring their learning to life by a rather more practical route, a route that remains with them because it is under their ownership.

With this preparation the students investigated a rather different style of writing, that of the first recorded 8th-century written epic poem in the English language – *Beowulf*. This represented a useful starting point in both an historical context of how 'news' has changed through the activities, and for study of a classical text.

A preliminary lesson had set the historical scene for the telling of the epic saga. Students chose how they wished to represent the information they were given, that would create for them a sense of being one of the warriors involved in the story. Their 'homework' was to bring in a blanket or duvet to their next lesson; they had the sense to suggest that a sleeping bag would be easier than the latter to bring to school and more comfortable to use; student power at work!

The lesson I wish to actually focus on is as follows: the students came equipped with blankets and sleeping bags, and the candles they had been able to make in an earlier lesson, so that we could light them as we re-created the sense of being in the Great Hall alongside the Storyteller, who is to speak of the past, the present and the future. We looked at the aims and direction of the lesson, and I explained the competences that were to be the focus for the day's work. The key competences here were learning to learn and managing information.

The lesson started by looking at the original text of the Beowulf story. A discussion was held as the students tried to make sense of what language they were looking at. They realized it was not 'romantic' in the style of the French they had become familiar with. They felt it was guttural and therefore moved towards suggesting it was German, Gaelic or Celtic. Their powers of deduction were very persuasive and well constructed. But ultimately, they were thrilled to discover that the language they were looking at, and hearing, was, in fact, their own!

We then looked at the map of Europe to see from where the Geats (Beowolf's countrymen) might have travelled, and then we found their destination: Denmark. This in turn led to speculation on how the warriors might have travelled there and the type of boat they had used and again fed back to the previous lesson when we had set the historical scene.

At this point I gave out their 'homework' sheet that was differentiated by the tasks they could choose to do. The sheet was based on the names of the characters to be found in the story and involved the correct pronunciation and for some, the spelling of the names. They also wanted to 'test' their parents' knowledge of Old English and devised various ways of dragging them into their 'homework'. (It is interesting to note that in our next lesson they were very happy to share how difficult their parents had found it and how 'superior' they were able to feel. One-upmanship never loses its thrill, however old you may be…!)

It was necessary to clear the classroom of furniture, which the students worked out together and did without any fuss, after having decided where best to store their bags and what layout would be the most successful, so that we could all sit or lie on the floor, wrapped in our bedding, waiting to hear the story as it unfolded. Teacher input was not required as they took decisions and worked together in the most efficient of ways.

The curtains were closed, the fire exit was seen to be clear (again, at their insistence) and then we were able to light the candles, pass out the textbooks and the story began. Although this was, in English curriculum terms, a speaking and listening exercise, that was only part of the lesson. After all, we were resting on herb-strewn straw; the walls of the Great Hall were covered with woven tapestries to keep out the chill winds and snow of winter. We were rested, having eaten well and drunk plenty. The Great Hall was filled with the smoke from the fire and the spiralling smoke chains of the candles. As brave warriors we were waiting to be entertained for the evening.

The language itself needed no help from me! The pictures created in the imagination of the students was based entirely on the phrases and sentences as the story unfolded. The artwork in the textbook we used was in itself enough to kindle the imagination of the students; they were very empty and sparse in detail and this in turn led to discussion about why they were so effective, so frightening...

Time passed quickly, the lesson drew to a close. The room was put back as we had found it and my warriors moved out of our time warp of 1,200 years ago and rushed off to play in the 21st century.

In my 'English' lesson I had strayed over subject boundaries, employed the competences of organizing situations, and literacy and communication, and used whatever means I could to create a lasting impression on the students in order to bring English to life. Within the lesson framework there was still a freedom for the youngsters to stamp their mark and make the learning their own. What more powerful teaching tool can we, as teachers, have at our fingertips?

Counting the Cost Module:
a typical lesson from an English specialist

Imogen Willgress

This lesson – a representative one from an English specialist – involves the following competences, bearing in mind that it is the process, not the outcome, that is at the core of the students' learning. During this lesson or two (our lessons are one hour) students will have been using a whole range of competences:

Literacy and Communication

- interpretation of written information and development of written skills
- listen and respond to others
- presentation and creative skills

Organizing Information

- ability to plan
- assessing relevance of information
- ability to meet deadlines
- use of ICT to organize information
- identify and make changes when required

Organizing Themselves / Relating to People

- being a co-operative team member
- knowledge of own strengths / weaknesses
- understanding of global citizenship
- being responsible for learning
- being a good team leader

Citizenship

- know values and ethics in our community
- understand how people, the legal system, the media and government operate
- the impact of technology on our lives
- valuing national and global identities

Emotional Intelligence / Empathy

- motivating oneself and others, harnessing emotions productively
- listen well to others, sensitivity to their feelings.

This module starts with the reading of the novel *Street Child* by Berlie Doherty, which is a story that investigates social conditions of life in the Victorian era.

Moving on from the Victorians we consider the thought that some children in the world today live a similar life and do not enjoy childhood as we know it. This leads to research into child labour and trading conditions in the world. Students are challenged and encouraged to do their individual research on suggested internet sites or be guided in the direction of a small range of books and magazines that are available. While investigating these sources we are able to look at the way information is presented in different media, discerning the purpose and audience of each piece, separating fact from opinion and looking for bias and reliable statistics.

The next stage is to share the information, and at this stage I present the situation where every member of the class must be part of a mixed group of between four and six (students are accustomed to working in mixed groups, knowing that having boys and girls together is likely to produce more variety of thought and ideas). Each student is expected to contribute to the group's presentation and each group is given the task of planning to deliver a presentation lasting approximately three minutes to teach the rest of us about their findings.

The groups will need 30–40 minutes to select their information and decide how to present it. They will have access to sugar paper, glue, scissors, plain paper, and so on, or basic props if they decide to opt for a dramatic interpretation. They will be encouraged to present their findings exactly how they want to.

Students often have far more original ideas than their teacher and in response to this task I have had very different presentations ranging from:

- drama, focusing on 'A day in the life of a cocoa farmer's child' – before Fairtrade became involved with the farm – and then afterwards;

- poems on the theme of child labour, recited by the group;

- presentation developed around a poster designed using information from the websites;

- PowerPoint presentations;

- media interview involving the group simulating an interview with representatives from all sides and the consumer who is ignorant about the origin of their purchases.

Students listen intently to each other and ask questions. They are encouraged to make constructive comments and note down information in response.

The next step is for the class to take home the information they have acquired, to share it and extend it with their family and then report back any more information they have gathered. One way to do this is by looking at labels of products to see if they are 'fair trade' or asking local shops what their awareness is or their commitment to the banning of child labour or the promotion of fair trade.

I will allow the students to lead us in the journey and sometimes this may mean being involved in ventures beyond the lesson. Following the discussion in one lesson the children decided that one way to create a real understanding of the issues being discussed was to become personally involved. They started a Fairtrade stall at afternoon breaks, selling Geo-bars: as a result of this lesson 18 months ago the students are still running this stall, making a profit that benefits a school in The Gambia, which they have 'adopted'.

Making the News Module – There are no limits
(An overview of a 'science' input across a full module)

Patrick Hazlewood

The rich possibilities within an integrated approach to curriculum delivery can be truly exciting for the teacher as well as for the student. The following outline provides a view of the areas covered by the students over the six-week module, Making the News. This represents the input of one teacher for four, one-hour periods over the six weeks but it is interconnected with the work of other colleagues teaching the same group. Science, mathematics, technology, philosophy, critical thinking, history, astronomy and English are all encountered albeit with the same teacher.

The module begins with the question, 'What is the news?' The usual array of answers leads to the statement, 'What is news to you may not be news to me; discuss'. This begins to encourage the students to realize that a simple idea that we all take for granted can be much more complex. The idea that news can be both immediate and infinite raises many more questions. For example, our relative lack of awareness as time moves on is illustrated by the question, 'What was happening on other parts of the planet when Jesus was born?' The idea that human history focuses on key events and ignores or minimizes other 'news' is an important one, but it also allows the development of critical questioning. Creating independent thinkers has, to an extent, been marginalized in the curriculum at Key Stage 3 and beyond.

In this module the ability to engage in debate is strongly developed through a process of raising questions that challenge the students' knowledge and understanding. Increasingly the teacher merges into the background accepting that he doesn't know all of the answers – far from it! The setting of the scene in this module is very much that it is a learning journey for everyone, teacher as well as student. While there are lesson plans the students know that they are negotiable. If an alternative line of enquiry emerges then the planned lesson goes and the class plan the replacement lesson. 'Homework' isn't actually set by the teacher; the group decides what is needed for the next lesson. For the continuation of their studies *at home* they will try to find answers to the questions that they themselves have posed.

The sequence of the next few lessons begins to unravel some of the mysteries uncovered by the concept of 'news'. Timelines are used to create a picture of news at important moments over the last 3,000 years, and the ways in which humans communicated this news are explored. Some of the work would be familiar to any Year 7 student (the ear, the eye, messages in pictures, written communication, TV, radio, mobile phones) but the Integrated Curriculum approach does not recognize limits. Therefore to understand the science of communication these students study the particulate nature of matter, calculate the speed of sound, discover how sound waves travel, investigate reflection, refraction, echoes, sound absorbency of materials and discuss emotional intelligence and 'sixth sense'. Angles, and calculations involving angles, are part of the 'discovery' but sine of the angle also comes in to help calculate refractive index.

In other parts of the story another teacher is looking at other aspects of news in the Norman Conquest. This provides an opportunity to look at some inventions in the past; in this case the trebuchet as a weapon designed to throw large objects at castle walls seems an obvious candidate.

The best way to understand, based on the research from previous lessons, is to build your own. The students embark on a design programme: first of all teams of designers and engineers are created; each person has a specific role depending on their strengths agreed by the group. The design is planned on paper, materials are ordered, measured, cut to size, structural matters such as angle of uprights to the base (for maximum strength) and methods of construction are agreed and the team go to the workshop to build the trebuchet.

Each team, after a period of trialling and modification, enters the self-directed competition to find out whose trebuchet is most effective. Finding out which one throws the projectile furthest is probably obvious, but the quality of the thinking that led to these designs demands a far more rigorous analysis of design strength and weakness. The competition included best design, best craftsmanship, strongest structure (measured by the load that the machine could support) and most original. It was the distance of 'projectile flight' aspect that was so surprising. The students realized that the flight of the projectile was actually an arc not a straight line and proceeded to try to calculate the distance travelled by the projectile. The final step resulted in the use of tangents drawn on the curve of trajectory. All of this was completely unaided: initially one group 'discovered' the idea and quickly shared it with the others. The significance of this finding for a class of 11 year olds is quite remarkable given that even able mathematicians are unlikely to try this work before the age of 15 or 16.

The story of the trebuchet did not stop here. The group decided that they needed to do more work on forces and motion to get a better understanding of their inventions. Force = mass x acceleration, force due to gravity and velocity/time graphs all came into *their* lesson plan. Not only did the whole group of mixed ability students understand, they could tackle (with confidence) questions from a GCSE paper (my idea, not theirs!).

This exciting journey drew to a close with the stars and the observation that looking at the night sky is actually looking at news that has taken millions of light years to arrive here. If events had happened there in the depths of space we would only now be seeing something that happened millions of years ago. The discussion around the universe and Stephen Hawking's work is a different concept to those original answers to the first question six weeks before… 'and what does making the news mean to you…?'

Chapter 8

The future of learning in the 21st century

Patrick Hazlewood

The learning journey that we, as a school, have made over the past four years has been remarkable. The original premise that the National Curriculum was acting as a blockage to the development and realization of the potential of our students has been proven. The pilot and, subsequently, the results in national tests and other internally set assessments have shown that the students do at least as well as in the 'normal' curriculum and, in many cases, much better. Objective results have been useful in the curriculum action research that we have undertaken, but it is the experience of living with this curriculum approach that has proved the most powerful validation of its success. The *Opening Minds* project has proved to be successful in each of the schools that piloted the competence based curriculum (RSA 2003). The real measure of success, however, lies in the high levels of confidence and capability of the learners.

Integrating the curriculum experience for the child makes sense. From the child's perspective all learning should be coherent, connected and continuous. Arriving at school, seeing the curriculum unfold rather like reading a book (preferably a very interesting one!), knowing that each of the 'teachers' that you meet on the way knows exactly what your story is about, must be the key to very powerful learning. As the journey progresses through the weeks and through the year the competences are clearly identified and developed in increasing depth. Learning to learn, managing information, managing situations and relating to other people are valued by all. As importantly, personal responsibility for one's own learning, taking risks and learning from mistakes, becoming effective in solving problems, developing a high level of communication expertise, developing understanding from a position of wanting to (rather than being told that you have to) and discovering that learning is fun all give meaning to the learning journey.

The barriers that have previously existed between subjects in the curriculum are artificial; why is it that secondary education is so different to primary education? Do children really change so radically in the summer vacation before their seventh year of compulsory schooling that the way that they are taught must also change radically? The issue of transition from primary school to secondary school has long been a thorny and time-consuming one. However, if the curriculum and *the approach to the delivery of the curriculum* were based on a common philosophy, with the learners' needs in this century at the heart of that philosophy, would there be a transition issue? Is it that the management structure of secondary education in schools is also a relic, post the 1944 Education Act? Is it the case that little thought has been given to what the internal organizational structure that supports the child's learning should look like, if the child were to be placed at the centre?

Further questions that emerge surround the 'one size fits all' National Curriculum. Schools are very effective at grouping children by ability and yet most enter exams at the same points in time, indeed the exams themselves become the justification for the curriculum and therefore the determining factor in where the learning journey goes. Tinkering with vocational routes versus academic routes does not recognize, nor provide for, the individual learners' needs at the time those needs arise. How then can the curriculum and the structural organization of schools provide our children with the educational experience that they need, and society needs them to have, if they are to be effective participants in the rapidly changing world in which we live?

Personalizing learning

Through the work that we have undertaken one thing has become very clear. If the system of education is to meet both the needs of the learner and the needs of society in the 21st century, then the curriculum and all that is associated with it must be focused on the needs of the individual. In the *Opening Minds* project the key elements for personalizing learning seem to be

- a clear understanding of the individual's learning styles and preferences;

- a working knowledge by the child and the teaching team of the personal strengths and weaknesses of the individual;

- knowing the person, who they are, where they come from and what their aspirations may be;

and

- listening to the individual's views on their learning.

Independent learning supported by ICT

This probably seems like a statement of the obvious. Communication has proved to be the single most important issue which, if I am honest, is not one that we have fully resolved. The language and intention of what we are trying to achieve is well received but the dismantling of the established 'way of doing things' is a fairly considerable hurdle. When we, with the RSA and others, first started this work it was perceived to be a significant risk to depart from the prescribed curriculum and the normal approach to teaching; it certainly felt like it! Recent shifts in government position have, however, been most encouraging. Charles Leadbeater's (2004) paper jointly published by Demos, the National College for School Leadership and DfES on Learning about Personalization supports the principles of what we have been trying to achieve. Together with David Hargreaves' (2004b) advocacy of the nine gateways to personalization of learning which are curriculum, advice and guidance, assessment for learning, learning to learn, school organization and design, workforce development, new technologies (ICT), mentoring and student voice, the tide may be ready to turn. However, Hargreaves (2004a) also points out that the DfES is concerned that the personalization of learning should not be identified with a return to child-centred philosophies of education, prevalent in the 1960s and 1970s.

The need for a clear and consistent philosophy of education is critical if schools and those within and around them are to feel empowered to educate effectively. The political will certainly seems to be moving in this direction. The publication of *Every Child Matters* (DfES 2004) is a very important step forwards. The centrality of personalized learning as both an aspiration and a philosophy provides a challenge for schools. By implication the door is now open to re-engineer our schools for the 21st century in a way that places the learner first. Perhaps we have reached the point described by Drucker (1993) where 'Western history (undergoes) a sharp transformation…and society rearranges itself (in terms of)… Basic values, social and political structures, its arts and its key institutions.'

Implications for teaching

From our experiences to date there can be little doubt that the role of the teacher must change if the approach to learning is to change. In the Integrated Curriculum work and the later evolution of the project we found that those who had been teaching for more than 20 years (pre-National Curriculum) had few problems in adjusting to the totally flexible approach. They did, however, have considerable training needs in terms of understanding the processes of learning and the strategies likely to be most effective in the classroom. Those new to the profession with unformed views on the 'right way to teach' proved to be adaptable, flexible and energetic in their approach to the new curriculum. Those who found the new approach so hard to accommodate were invariably trained in the National Curriculum years.

However, if the pathways to a personalized curriculum are to be properly implemented then teacher training will need to be re-thought. The subject specialist may remain important in the later stages of secondary education and in the delivery of exam courses, but in the first three years the ability to span a range of related subjects with confidence seems essential. Understanding how a child learns, learning styles, experience of a wide range of teaching strategies and understanding how to assess *for* learning should form a part of the newly qualified teacher's portfolio.

This however is only the beginning. Teachers in the school of the 21st century will need to be more adaptable and engage in continuous professional development. This is not a criticism of what I regard as a very highly skilled and capable profession, but a reflection that as our learners exceed our expectations the culture of professional evolution must be in place to support them.

The professional teacher must be properly equipped to become a thinking and reflective practitioner able to make autonomous judgements in complex and holistic settings. This will require schools to engage with the next major challenge, that of re-engineering the way the school is managed.

Implications for school management

There is still a tendency for schools to manage through a hierarchical structure which has the effect of creating a bureaucratic organization. This is perhaps not surprising given that the intention is to emphasize conformity, uniformity and, ultimately, efficiency and accountability. This runs counter to what Darling-Hammond (1993) refers to as professional prerequisites, that is, professional preparation, knowledge for decision making, ethical and codified standards of practice and attention to the unique needs of clients. In the wider scheme of things centralization of power and decision making invariably disempowers those who actually deliver the curriculum and engage with the children. Perhaps the time has come for schools to take a radical look at how they manage and why they manage in the way that they do. If the most important relationship in the school is at the point where teacher and child interact, then the school philosophy and management structure must support that; indeed it becomes the reason for its existence rather than a collection of things that need managing.

The fundamental 'conversation' in any school should revolve around teaching and learning. In an ideal school scenario there would simply be a collection of professional teachers engaged in a collegiate approach to meeting the needs of their clients. There should be no need for a management hierarchy that proliferates almost as a matter of course – heads of departments, seconds in department, and so on. An effective body of *professional* teachers fully involved in the direction and organization of the learning environment, properly supported by an administrative team and other paraprofessionals, should be quite capable of managing themselves. There would need to be effective peer review systems in place that provided mutual critical support. Ensuring that the team of professionals remained at the forefront of professional practice would be taken for granted and that knowledge management (Caldwell 2004) was a concept both subscribed to and enacted. Caldwell defines *knowledge management* as 'the creation, dissemination and utilization of knowledge for the purpose of improving teaching and learning and to guide decision making in every domain of professional practice'. As part of this project the distribution of leadership has proved to be highly effective and has realized a considerable growth in the professional capability of those involved.

Visions and partnership

There are many lessons from our work on the *Opening Minds* project. Probably the most fundamentally important one is that engagement in the process of learning is a partnership in which both child and teacher are learning together. There are times when the roles become reversed; this reversal is easier for some to accept than others. Change, in terms of the traditional understanding of the role of the teacher, is a sensitive issue in that the teacher may feel vulnerable or exposed. Care for the person and clarity of explanation about why the change is necessary are therefore vital. From the position of the teacher isolated in the subject-specific classroom, we found that a far higher degree of professional interaction, sharing of ideas and experiences took place. This in turn has led to a willingness to be exposed because the experience is not at all threatening.

From this micro perspective there emerges a view of the future evolution of schools. 'School' itself may not be the most useful term; it implies that this is where learning happens when in reality it can happen anywhere. It also acts to create a concept of a group of people distinct from other groups of people in other 'schools'. The future transformation of education may well embrace the idea of learning communities but it must include an understanding that working across learning communities will be vital to effective and sustainable development. Sharing knowledge, sharing ideas and effective practice will help to ensure a dynamic profession fully focused on the high achievement of the individual child.

Leadership will still be an essential ingredient in creating the conditions for transformation and further evolution. In terms of collegiality, however, different individuals may emerge as leaders at different times. Real leadership is, in part, about creating the conditions that allow this to happen. For visions to be successfully realized they must be shared ones owned by the learning community. The distribution of leadership through the organization brings with it higher levels of motivation, commitment and autonomy. Equally important is the notion that leadership can be distributed across schools who work closely in partnership

Our work began with the needs of the learner in the 21st century and the development of a competency based curriculum that created rich and diverse opportunities for a very powerful learning environment. We have emerged with a very successful, very exciting and very rewarding curriculum but have also opened the proverbial 'can of worms'. Further growth in curriculum and professional terms must bring about the next phase of transformation, sooner and not later. That transformation must address the personalization of learning and will transform the organizational culture. Plans will include all adults employed in the organization, not just teachers, acting as mentors to individual children.

Assessment for learning, already in place, will change the way in which we report to parents. Reports will probably be a continual three-way dialogue between the child, the mentor and the parent as an online summative document with all assessments and related targets being updated on a monthly basis.

Homework, as a thing that teachers do to you, must go. In its place 'own learning', that extends beyond the time at school but that is interconnected and cross-disciplinary allowing the learner greater freedom for personalization of that learning. Traditional management structures, already considerably modified, will change further to bring about the conditions for 'extended' professionals to take ownership of the learning environment. To allow this to happen workplace transformation will require a revolution in terms of which tasks are undertaken by whom. The boundary between the primary and secondary school must be removed. The child has a right to a continuous and coherent education; artificial boundaries for reasons of age or geography must not be allowed to impede the learning journey either for the child or the other inhabitants of the learning communities.

The radical step that we took in 2001 now seems only a small one compared with what lies before us!

Appendix 1

The Year 7 Curriculum Handbook

It is not the purpose of this book to provide the details of putting together the subject areas of the six modules and the day-by-day learning of our students. Each of the initial RSA pilot schools, and those that followed later, has had to find its own way of achieving the necessary blend of elements to suit their own school. This appendix therefore provides an abridged version of only the introduction to our *Year 7 Curriculum Handbook*, to provide a guide to the ethos of the system used at St John's School.

Teaching and Learning

 If the child cannot learn in the way that you teach, can you teach in the way the child learns?

It has long been recognized that most students can achieve greater success if their education engages them and taps into their individual learning style. With thought and planning it can engage the kinesthetic learner, challenge the gifted and talented, and readily provide alternative routes for those who find it difficult to commit ideas in writing. As students are becoming more aware of their own style of learning, they need to have the opportunity to use these strengths to achieve success. From this position of strength they will then be more confident to experiment, take risks and further develop their skills for learning.

Learning should:

- be clearly focused with targets that are relevant and achievable;
- engage all students by making the tasks accessible and manageable (differentiation);
- be negotiated to suit the strengths of the student;
- be paced with students knowing the steps they need to make progress;
- develop the joy of learning through success and experience;
- include outcomes which challenge all students;

- teach the student how to...;
- create links within the whole curriculum experience of each student so that repetition can be avoided, freeing up time for greater depth and rigour.

We can often extend students as they see the relevance of their learning in the creation of a range of outcomes. As the Year 7 Curriculum has developed we have become more aware of the potential for developing a far wider range of skills than we previously recognized. It is critical that these skills are made explicit and transferable in various contexts. The teacher will need to lead and direct this skills transfer initially.

The key skills are:

- Literacy and Communication
- Citizenship
- Organizing Self and Relating to People
- Numeracy and Problem Solving
- Managing Information.

Some aspects of these competences are inextricably linked to the learning process while others are opportunities that can be provided with some planning, for example thinking systematically can be tied in with creating a planning sheet, but if this was done in pairs or by a small group of students they could then assist each other.

The skills are developed through the approaches we use to deliver the curriculum. What is most important is that it is made explicit to students what skills they are focusing upon. Good practice is to identify the skills at the start of the lesson on the posters in each classroom or by recognizing them within the task instructions. Students have a copy of the competences in their planners and should be able to take a task and identify which skills they can develop.

The Year 7 skills based curriculum is a key focus for the strategic plan of the school and embeds the school ethos firmly in the curriculum structure. As each year has progressed we have modified approaches in line with evaluation feedback and will continue to do so.

Management structure

The Year 7 Curriculum is overseen by the Year 7 curriculum co-ordinator, who in turn reports to the KS3 strategy manager and then directly to SMT. The directorate KS3 co-ordinators are responsible for contributing to the structure, content and management of their directorate input within the modules. They play a significant part in the direction the curriculum takes and the success of the skills based approach. Each directorate has identified the skills and content of the modules they will be delivering and reporting on. Moderation and cross-moderation procedures will happen within the normal school programme. Financial overview is with the KS3 strategy manager, individual directors will submit bids for materials and resources for Year 7.

Professional development

There will be additional support and monitoring of delivery of the competences and the differentiation of the curriculum to meet the needs of students. In line with this there will be additional professional development for ITTs, NQTs and new staff to the school covering the ethos and expectations of the directorate. This will take place formally in the early part of the school year and informally as needs arise. Any member of staff wanting additional advice or support should contact the Year 7 curriculum co-ordinator.

As the *Opening Minds* curriculum approaches gain momentum nationally any developments will become agenda items within the meetings cycle. KS3 co-ordinators will contribute to the agenda to raise issues needing discussion and resolution. Extra-curricular activities leading on from the curriculum should be brought to the meetings so that their educational value can be extended and built upon by direct links from other areas of the curriculum.

Assessment marking and recording

The marking policy is clearly set out and should be applied to both skills assessment and curriculum content. As data will be held on Assessment Manager it will be accessible for staff in whatever format required. As students progress through the school this data is again accessible to ensure effective transition year on year and between the key stages.

Assessment for learning

 It is the process, not the outcome, that is at the core of the student's learning.

National Curriculum assessments will take place every module, that is once within each six-week block. Directorates should identify the task and ensure completion before the end of the module; this will be recorded on an OMR. Where possible formative assessment strategies should be used to inform and guide students to make it clear what is needed for further progress.

Assessment of competences can be built into the learning experiences and need not be teacher driven. Self-evaluation and peer assessment are useful strategies, especially if they involve students developing and using the criteria for marking. Again this can be done prior to completion of a task so that it becomes a formative process.

Reporting will take place informally, as a 'snapshot' transition review in November when a letter is sent home recording how the student has settled into the tutor group, his/her attitude to learning and general behaviour. This is followed by a parents' evening in early February and an end of year report where tutors will report on overall competence levels based upon the data staff provide over the year. This will be stored in Assessment Manager for directorates to access rather than having double input.

Teachers are expected to keep a record of all assessments and NC levels in their mark book or directorate recording system.

Monitoring

The normal school systems for monitoring will be in place:

- Lesson observations by directors, ELT and SMT;
- Paired observation to share expertise with other members of staff;
- Student end-of-module reviews;
- Review of tutor log books and student planners;
- Data review by Assessment Manager.

Use of data

Data will be collected on transition to give an overview of the student pastorally and academically. At Induction, attitude to learning, multiple intelligences and self-esteem will be collated and available as both a teaching group profile as well as individual profiles.

Transition

The transition documents are stored in the pupil files; these contain additional information to the standard KS2–3 data. In particular there are details on literacy and numeracy as well as particular learning needs. See tutor folder at the front of the filing cabinet for summative information from the pastoral database and KS3 co-ordinators for literacy and numeracy information.

Assessment Manager

Data from NC levels at KS2 with chronological, reading and spelling ages will be available in September. As the year progresses assessments will be entered via OMRs. Two competences will be assessed in each module and National Curriculum assessments will be made termly. There will be a hard copy of all this data in the tutor group folder at the front of the files in the principal tutor's office. Summaries will be made available on the shared area of the network.

Data will be collected and disseminated to:

- Tutors for parents' evening and reports;
- Students by the teachers as formative advice in normal lessons;
- Parents as snapshot transition review in November;
- At parents' evening mid year;
- In the end-of-year report;
- For teachers, directors and SMT as part of normal data processing;
- By SENCO and tutors as individual student's mapping process.

Support and further professional development

In recognizing the change in approach and methodology, for many teachers advice and support can be sought from more experienced colleagues or the Year 7 curriculum co-ordinator on a one-to-one basis. Formal support will be provided within the CPD pitched to suit the needs of teachers, that is NQTs and new teachers.

Self-monitoring and self-evaluation

The tutor as learning manager will engage the students in reviewing their performance at the end of each module and help set appropriate targets for personal development within the next module. These will be the students' key foci although individual teachers will advise students on how to achieve higher levels of performance within subject specific skills.

Issues arising within the tutor group can be highlighted and actioned using the tutor group log. While confidential comments cannot be included, general observations which would improve the learning environment should be noted.

Through the normal cycle of meetings when the teaching team meet, students and learning should be on the agenda. The teaching team can then agree common strategies and approaches. Observations and monitoring procedures should feed into this process.

The student and parental voice should be noted by the tutor from student reviews and parental contacts, this can then be fed back to the teaching team.

Differentiation

It is critical that all learning tasks and experiences are differentiated to meet the needs of the groups as a whole as well as meeting individual needs. There will be data available in the shared area and in the tutor group folder in the principal tutor's office.

If students are unable to access the curriculum they become disaffected and behavioural issues arise. Students who feel valued and engaged will perform significantly better. The student needs register has been significantly extended. It will identify the key issues regarding each student including IEPs, level of need, specific conditions, gifted and talented, students who are withdrawn, accessing Lexia, requiring additional time in tests, and so on.

The student perspective

All teachers should access the student needs register and keep it updated as additional information is issued on specific students. It is critical that all students are set very high expectations and that they are given the opportunities to achieve these goals regardless of any special need. This will require a high level of differentiation and should engage the student in the process of target-setting and realistic outcomes in line with ability. Once the student has this grasp of relating outcome to their specific needs they will be empowered to suggest aspects of differentiation which could enable them to make greater progress. Wherever possible those recognized as gifted and talented should be nurtured and challenged to develop their enjoyment of learning as well as level of achievement.

All students with individual education plans should make these known to the teachers and must be regularly reviewed and signed. If a student is not doing this it is the learning manager's and the teacher's responsibility to manage this. Feedback from the teachers is critical to making the IEP relevant and worthwhile. This should either be fed back via the IEP or directly with the TA, tutor or SENCO. Where a TA is supporting the class their role is to facilitate learning and support the students and staff. They are experienced in managing the learning of students and as such should be part of the negotiation process when looking at the learning and assessment of students as well as setting appropriate targets. They are often the people who see the whole student across a range of curriculum areas. Requests for additional support for students should go via the directorate to the SENCO using the referral form. When a student is posing behavioural problems, initially support should be sought from the directorate team of that subject area. Most directorates have rewards and sanctions in place; if additional advice is needed see the Year 7 curriculum co-ordinator.

Learning issues

If a student is failing to make progress after normal classroom strategies have been employed then a referral should be made to the SENCO or Year 7 curriculum co-ordinator and advice sought. A review of teaching strategies and 'round robins' will be undertaken prior to meeting with the student and/or parents to resolve the issues.

Extended learning

A progression of the homework / work@home.fun is to develop the idea of student ownership of their learning beyond the classroom. Extended learning is directed by the teacher and developed by the student. Those students who have not developed the ability to organize themselves or their learning will need to be shown how to do so and will need the normal structures if they fail to complete their tasks. Conversely recognition should be given to the student who has taken advice and developed their own structure and outcome. As with all things students should be made aware of our expectations that a minimum of one hour is spent on extended learning each night. Students who exceed this should be shown how to focus and manage tasks.

School dress code

All students will wear correct school dress as indicated in the planner; normal sanctions must be followed if students don't comply.

Enjoyment of learning and academic expectations

The cornerstone of this curriculum is the engagement of the student by the provision of exciting and challenging experiences. This will be reflected in the students' motivation to learn and thus move them towards becoming independent learners. Another keystone of this curriculum is to set very high expectations and enable students to achieve them. All students in Year 6 have, at their primary school, achieved a high level of independent working – we should build upon this and not create dependence. Many students experience a dip in standards of presentation as we increase the pace of work to a point where they cannot maintain the standard of presentation in which they have previously taken great pride.

Behaviour

The students are aware of the high standards we expect; everyone must maintain these standards. This should be addressed as a teaching group issue and the students should be involved in raising and maintaining a positive working atmosphere. Students with significant behavioural issues will be referred to the learning manager, principal tutor and SENCO. Engagement of outside agencies will be an option should other internal support strategies fail to resolve the situation.

Rewards

In the transition phase students usually respond well to our normal variety of rewards. They value merits and should be encouraged by recognition of their efforts or the standards they achieved. Merits are collected and bronze, silver, gold and platinum certificates are awarded. Further merits achieve a headteacher's commendation. Many students value a note in their planner for good work and enjoy taking positive yellow referrals home to their parents; these are later filed.

Sanctions

Use as wide a range of sanctions as possible so that students have time to respond before they require punitive sanctions. Self-management and tutor group responsibility should be engaged to resolve issues.

- Serious misbehaviour should be brought to the director's attention and subject specific strategies should be employed initially.

- Loss of breaks and lunchtimes can be informal deterrents or formalized as lunchtime detentions run by directorates. Should this not succeed in improving the situation refer to the learning manager and principal tutor.

- Lower School detentions and after school detentions are employed when other sanctions have been tried and failed.

- Yellow referrals and use of emergency cover are serious sanctions and result in a letter going to parents and directors.

Appendix 2

Example module outline – Being Unique

Geography	Drama
Where they come from. Maps, journeys around maps and grid references. Compass directions.	Teamwork 'It was Terrifying'. Space, body language, monologue, group-work.
Maths	**IT**
Use of statistics/data, graphs – based on family, class surveys, government spending.	PowerPoint skills – presentation on 'Themselves'.
Art	**DT**
Tonal observations of themselves. Relief portraits in clay. Evaluation.	Unique properties of materials. Newspaper. Evaluation – transportation.
MFL (Ger)	**MFL (Fr)**
Numbers, where we live, info on people, towns, countries, family vocab.	Brothers, sisters, where they live, birthdays, ages.

Science	History
Cells, structure, scientific enquiry, microscopes, biological investigations – growth of pollen tubes. Human reproduction, body changes, menstrual cycle, breeding.	Use of evidence. Mark Pullen, Tutankhamun – theories, reconstruction. Analysis – presentation by students. Bog Bodies, Tollund Man (Denmark).
PE	**English**
Teamwork. Contribution as citizen. Ability to plan, identifying/changing.	Autobiography – *Boy* photo game, research, Milestones, Red Letter Days, personal shields, poetry of family. Survey and interviews.
Music	**RE**
Mood, atmosphere, structures, keys, 'unique' quality of sound, notes.	Identity and experience. Who we are.

Appendix 3

The RSA *Opening Minds* competences

Developing a competence-led curriculum

In *Opening Minds* five categories of competences are proposed. Each category contains a number of individual competences, which are expressed in terms of what a school student could achieve having progressed through the curriculum.

Competences for Learning

Students would:

- understand how to learn, taking account of their preferred learning styles, and understand the need to, and how to, manage their own learning throughout life

- have learned, systematically, to think

- have explored and reached an understanding of their own creative talents, and how best to make use of them

- have learned to enjoy and love learning for its own sake and as part of understanding themselves

- have achieved high standards in literacy, numeracy and spatial understanding

- have achieved high standards of competence in handling information and communications technology and understand the underlying processes.

Competences for Citizenship

Students would:

- have developed an understanding of ethics and values, how personal behaviour should be informed by these, and how to contribute to society

- understand how society, government and business work, and the importance of active citizenship

- understand cultural and community diversity, in both national and global contexts, and why these should be respected and valued

- understand the social implications of technology
- have developed an understanding of how to manage aspects of their own lives, and the techniques they might use to do so – including managing their financial affairs.

Competences for Relating to People

Students would:

- understand how to relate to other people in varying contexts in which they might find themselves, including those where they manage, or are managed by, others; and how to get things done
- understand how to operate in teams, and their own capacities for filling different team roles
- understand how to develop other people, whether as peer or teacher
- have developed a range of techniques for communicating by different means, and understand how and when to use them
- have developed competence in managing personal and emotional relationships
- understand, and be able to use, varying means of managing stress and conflict.

Competences for Managing Situations

Students would:

- understand the importance of managing their own time, and have developed preferred techniques for doing so
- understand what is meant by managing change, and have developed a range of techniques for use in varying situations
- understand the importance both of celebrating success and managing disappointment, and ways of handling these
- understand what is meant by being entrepreneurial and initiative-taking, and how to develop capacities for these
- understand how to manage risk and uncertainty, the wide range of contexts in which these will be encountered, and techniques for managing them.

Competences for Managing Information

Students would:

- have developed a range of techniques for accessing, evaluating and differentiating information and have learned how to analyse, synthesize and apply it
- understand the importance of reflecting and applying critical judgement, and have learned how to do so.

Glossary

AC	Alternative Curriculum; changed to Year 7/8 Curriculum in 2003
ADHD	Attention deficit hyperactivity disorder
A/S	Advanced subsidiary level – an external examination usually taken as the first stage of Advanced level qualifications
Brain Gym®	A system of small sitting stationary exercises that relax students for a few moments' respite during periods of high concentration
CPD	Continuing professional development
CSE Mode 3	Certificate of Secondary Education using a syllabus designed by the school but assessed externally
Director	The school's term for the head/leader/manager of a subject
Directorate	The subject team led by the director
DT	Design and technology
ELT	English language teaching
GCE	General Certificate of Education
GCSE	General Certificate of Secondary Education
HMI	Her Majesty's Inspector, an independent government body which makes independent judgements about all activities in schools
IBP	Individual behaviour plan
IC	Integrated Curriculum; changed to Alternative Curriculum in 2003
ICT	Information and communication technology
IEP	Individual education plan
INSET	In-service education and training for teachers
IQEA	Improving Quality of Education for All
ITT	Initial teacher training
Key Stage	A period of education terminating in an externally marked examination
KS3	Key Stage 3 – students aged 11–14
KS4	Key Stage 4 – students aged 14–16
KS5	Key Stage 5 – students aged 16–19

LEA	Local education authority
MFL	Modern foreign languages – a directorate which teaches French, German and Spanish at St John's
MI	Multiple intelligences
NC	National Curriculum
NQT	Newly qualified teacher – teachers in their first year of teaching
Ofsted	Office for Standards in Education – the government body concerned with the quality of teaching and learning inspections in schools
OMR	Optical mark reader
PE	Physical education
RE	Religious education
RSA	Royal Society for the encouragement of Arts, Manufactures and Commerce
SATs	Standard assessment tests taken at the end of Key Stage 3
SENCO	Special educational needs co-ordinator
SMT	Strategic management team
TA	Teaching assistant
The Book	The journal (log book) carried by a student from lesson to lesson
TQM	Total quality management

References

Association for Supervision and Curriculum Development (1999) *Preparing Our Schools for the 21st Century*, ASCD, Alexandria

Bacon, Francis (1625) *Essays*

Bayliss, Valerie (1998a) *Redefining Work*, RSA, London

Bayliss, Valerie (1998b) *Redefining Schooling*, RSA, London

Bayliss, Valerie, Brown, Joanna and James, Lesley (1998) *Redefining the Curriculum*, RSA, London

Beare, H., Caldwell, B.J. and Millikan, R.H. (1989) *Creating an Excellent School: Some New Management Techniques*, Routledge, London

Bowring-Carr, C. and West-Burnham, J. (1994) *Managing Quality in Schools – A Training Manual*, Longman, Harlow

Caldwell, Brian (2004) *Re-imagining the Self-Managing School*, Specialist Schools Trust, London

Caldwell, Brian and Spinks, J. (1988) *The Self-Managing School*, Falmer Press, Lewes

Cowelti, G. (1993) *Challenges and Achievements in American Education*, ASCD, Alexandria

Crabtree, L., Glew, M., Gunn, P., Surridge, M. and Watts, M. (1996) *Human Resources for Advanced GNVQ*, Collins, London. Reprinted by permission of HarperCollins Publishers Ltd. © Crabtree, Glen, Gunn, Surridge and Watts, 1996

Darling-Hammond L. (1990) 'Teacher Professionalism: Why and How?' in Lieberman A (ed.) *Schools as Collaborative Cultures: Creating the Future Now*, Falmer Press, New York

Darling-Hammond L. (1993) *Progress Toward Professionalism in Teaching*, ASCD Yearbook (1993), ASCD, Alexandria

DfES (2004) *Every Child Matters*, HMSO, London

Drucker, P.F. (1993) *Post-capitalist Society*, Harper Business, New York

Ellyard, P. (1997) *Developing a Learning Culture*, virtual paper presented to Australian Council for Education Administration

Elmore, R. (1990) *Restructuring School*, Jossey-Bass, Oakland, Calif.

Evans, D. (1990) *People, Communication and Organizations*, Pitman, London

Fullan, Michael (1988) *What's Worth Fighting for in the Principalship*, Ontario Public School Teachers' Federation, Toronto

Fullan, Michael and Hargreaves, A. (1991) *What's Worth Fighting For?: Working together for your school*, Ontario Public School Teachers' Federation, Toronto

Gardner, Howard (1983) *Frames of Mind*, Fontana, London

Goleman, Daniel (1995) *Emotional Intelligence: Why it can matter more than IQ*, Bantam, New York

Handy, Charles (1994) *The Empty Raincoat: Making Sense out of the Future*, Hutchinson, London

Hargreaves, David (2001) *A Future for the School Curriculum*, Speech at the RSA

Hargreaves, David (2004a) *Learning for Life*, The Policy Press, Bristol

Hargreaves, David (2004b) *Personalised Learning: next steps in working laterally*, Specialist Schools Trust, London

Hazlewood, Patrick (1985) 'More about Chemistry with a World Studies Perspective', *School Science Review* 66, 236, 539–543

Hazlewood, Patrick (1988) 'Global Perspectives in Chemistry' in Pike, G. and Selby, D. *Global Teacher, Global Learner*, Hodder & Stoughton, Sevenoaks

Hazlewood, Patrick (1994) 'The influence of appraisal on the middle management of secondary schools', unpublished PhD thesis, University of Exeter

Hazlewood, Patrick (1997) *St John's School and Community College Mission Statement*, The School Prospectus

Hazlewood, Patrick (2005) '*Homework row helps pupils study*', reported in *Times Educational Supplement* 28.01.05 (p. 10)

HMCI Report (1997) *Effective Schools*, HMSO London

HMI (1988) *Secondary Schools*: an Appraisal by HMI, HMSO, London

HMSO (1967) *Children and their Primary Schools: A report for the Central Advisory Council for Education* (The Plowden Report), HMSO, London

Hooker, R. (1594) *On the Laws of Ecclesiastical Polity*

Hopkins, D., Ainscow M. and West, M. (1994) *School Improvement in an Era of Change*, Cassell, London

Huberman, M. (1992) 'Critical Introduction' in Fullan, M. *Successful School Improvement*, Open University Press, Milton Keynes

Kamil, C. (2003) *Young Children Continue to Reinvent Arithmetic – 2nd grade implications for Piaget's Theory*, Teachers College Press, USA

Key Stage 3 National Strategy (2004; 1 September) http://edunet.iow.gov.uk, web page

Kotter, J. (1990) 'What Leaders Really Do', *Harvard Business Review*, 90 (3)

Lawton, D. (1973) *Social Change, Educational Theory and Curriculum Planning*, Routledge & Kegan Paul, London

Leadbeater, Charles (2004) *Learning about Personalisation: how can we put the learner at the heart of the education system?*, DfES Publications, Nottingham

Leithwood, K.A. (1992) 'The Move Towards Transformational Leadership', *Educational Leadership* 49 (5), 8–12

Maclure, Stuart (1988) *Education Reformed*, Hodder & Stoughton, Sevenoaks

Mercer, Neil (2000) *Words and Mind: how we use language to think together*, Routledge, London

Miliband, David, Minister of State for Schools Standards (2004) Speech to the North of England Conference

Mitchell, D.E. and Tucker, S. (1992) 'Transformational Leadership' in Drucker, P. (1993) *Transformational Leadership*. Reported in SIN *Research Matters*, Institute of Education, Spring 1998. No 8

Murgatroyd, S. and Morgan, C. (1993) *Total Quality Management and the School*, Open University Press, Buckingham

Murphy, J. (1991) *Restructuring Schools: Capturing and Assessing the Phenomena*, Teachers College Press, New York

Ofsted (1997) *Report: St John's School*, HMI

Pajak, E. (1993) 'Change and Continuity in Supervision and Leadership' in Cowelti , G. (see above)

Rogers, B. (1997), *Cracking the Hard Class: Strategies for Managing the Harder than Average Class*, Scholastic Australia, Lisarow, NSW

RSA (1999) *Opening Minds: Education for the 21st Century*, RSA, London

RSA (2003) *Opening Minds: Taking Stock*, RSA, London

Rudduck, J., Chaplain, R. and Wallace, G. (1996) *School Improvement, What Can Pupils Tell Us?*, David Fulton Publication

Smith, Alistair (2003) *Accelerated Learning – a user's guide*, Network Educational Press, Stafford

Southworth, G. (1994) 'The Learning School' in Ribbins, P. and Burridge, P. *Improving Education*, Cassell, London

Stedman, A.R. (1944) *A History of Marlborough Grammar School*, C.H. Woodward, Devizes

Stenhouse, Lawrence (1975) *An Introduction to Curriculum Research and Development*, Heinemann, London. Reprinted by permission of Harcourt Education

Sternberg, Robert (1997) *Thinking Styles*, Cambridge University Press, Cambridge

Stoll, L. (1999) *Realising Our Potential: Building Capacity for Lasting Improvement*. Keynote presentation to the Twelfth International Congress for School Effectiveness and Improvement, San Antonio, Texas, January 1999

Stoll, L. and Fink, D. (1996) *Changing our Schools: Linking School Effectiveness and School Improvement*, Open University Press, Buckingham

21st Century Learning Initiative (1997), *Executive Summary; initiative synthesis*, Washington, DC

West-Burnham, J. (1997) *Managing Quality in Schools* (2nd edn), Pitman Publishing, London

Acknowledgements

The authors of this book have greatly appreciated the huge amount of guidance and support offered by the Royal Society for the Encouragement of Arts, Manufactures and Commerce (RSA) and the Innovations Unit of the Department for Education and Skills.

Thanks must also go to Max More for the photographs throughout the book; the parents and students of Years 7 and 8 over the last four years; and perhaps most of all our colleagues – the teaching and support staff at St John's School and Community College – without whom none of this would have been possible.

Index